Using Fractions, Decimals and Percent

LEVEL C

by Christine Losq

A Houghton Mifflin Company
Wilmington, Massachusetts

Acknowledgments: The development of this unit was inspired by many people—educational researchers, students, and teachers like you. All have a goal in common —to create classrooms that are communities of learners where students develop flexible problem-solving strategies, dependable mental math skills, and communication skills for life-long learning.

We are infinitely grateful to those students who generously shared their ideas with others. In particular, we wish to thank teacher Robin Levy at Jordan Middle School in Palo Alto, California, who has inspired students with her creative assignments. We also salute teacher Kris Callahan and her students at Jordan who shared their work with us, so we can all learn from them.

Cover: Photo by David S. Waitz. Design and production by Bill SMITH STUDIO: Brian Kobberger, Art Director; Sandra Schmitt, Designer; Justine Price, Photo Editor.

Text: Design and production by Flying Pages, Inc.

Illustrations: Susan Miller, 125–133, S-10. Additional illustrations copyright ©Nicolas Losq. Used with permission of the artist.

Copyright © 1998 by Great Source Education Group, Inc. All rights reserved.

Permission is hereby granted to teachers to reprint or photocopy only the *Teacher Resources* and *Student Activity Pages* in classroom quantities for use in their classes with accompanying Great Source material, provided each copy made shows the copyright notice. Such copies may not be sold and further distribution is expressly prohibited. Except as authorized above, prior written permission must be obtained from Great Source Education Group to reproduce or transmit this work or portions thereof in any other form or by any other electronic or mechanical means, including any information storage or retrieval system, unless expressly permitted by federal copyright law. Address inquiries to Permissions, Great Source Education Group, 181 Ballardvale Street, Wilmington, MA 01887.

Printed in the United States of America

International Standard Book Number: 0-669-44450-2

1 2 3 4 5 6 7 8 9 0 PO 02 01 00 99 98 97

URL address: http://www.greatsource.com/

PREFACE

This unit evolved over a number of years in fifth and sixth grade classrooms to meet the learning needs of adolescents. Each year, our students came into the classroom with plenty of rote knowledge of place value and rote practice with decimal computation. However, they often did not demonstrate the mastery we wanted to see. They were not connecting computation to ideas of number theory. They were not constructing those generalizations about how numbers work that would prepare them for algebraic thinking. They also were not making the connections that are essential for developing efficient consumer skills.

We set out to create learning vehicles that would help our middle schoolers reach for a new level of mathematical thinking. We decided that it was time to put students into the driver's seat, to require them to apply critical thinking skills to their number manipulations, and to extend all that experience with decimal computation to new learning with fractions and percents.

The lessons and projects in this unit are designed to help students understand how decimals, fractions and percent interconnect. We designed the lessons to build on
- language connections to mathematics
- math connections that require critical thinking
- peer interactions

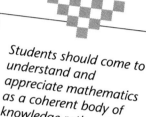

Students should come to understand and appreciate mathematics as a coherent body of knowledge rather than a vast, perhaps bewildering, collection of isolated facts and rules. . . .

It is no longer necessary or useful to devote large portions of instructional time to performing routine computations by hand. Other mathematical experiences for middle school students deserve far more emphasis.
NCTM Standards
pages 91, 94

As every experienced teacher knows, adolescents need not only challenging and engaging learning tasks but also opportunities to interact with their peers. In our experience, the role of the teacher shrinks on the landscape of fifth and sixth graders as the role of their peers grows. We capitalize on this reality by involving students in peer interactions and cooperative learning situations where they become resources for each other.

Students have opportunities to use both large and small motor skills, to interact with their peers, to develop a habit of reflecting on emerging patterns, to use patterns to make generalizations, and to develop their number sense in problem-solving settings.

In our classroom, we combine computation facilitated by calculators and daily practice with mental math strategies. In this way, no student is excluded from those learning tasks that build conceptual understanding of numbers and number theory. We foster computational competence with 15-minute warm-ups that support the conceptual explorations. In this way, students have regular and ongoing opportunities to practice computation as they develop grade-level appropriate math concepts like number theory and algebraic thinking.

The activities, lessons and projects in this unit work together as an effective, balanced teaching model that addresses a variety of strengths and learning needs. Individual lessons build understanding of concepts and skills. Projects help students discover how all of these concepts and skills are interrelated in the larger mathematical picture. As students work on projects, you will be able to assess developmental progress; you will be able to coach individual students and small groups; you will develop a picture of the whole child for each of your students as you evaluate their work.

Christine Losq

TABLE OF CONTENTS

Welcome to MathZones	vii

USING MATHZONES   1

Using this Unit	2
Using the Lesson Plan	4
Skills Matrix	6
Classroom Organization	8
Materials	9
Thinking and Talking Math	10
Four-Step Writing Plan	11
Using Math Journals	12
Teaching with Projects	13
Integrating Mathematics into the Curriculum	14
Teacher Talk	15
Family Involvement	16
Assessment	17

1 • WHAT DO YOU KNOW ABOUT DECIMALS   19

Lesson 1: Write About Decimals—Assessment 1	20

2 • LAUNCH THE STOCK MARKET PROJECT   25

Project Overview	26
Lesson 2: Business Basics	28
Lesson 3: Follow a Stock	34

3 • DECIMAL CONCEPTS   37

Lesson 4: Decimal Place Value Patterns	38
Lesson 5: Read and Round decimals	42
Lesson 6: Read Decimals	46
Lesson 7: Compare and Order Decimals	48
Lesson 8: Estimate and order Decimals—Assessment 2	50

4 • FRACTIONS, DECIMALS AND MONEY — 55

- Lesson 9: Make a Time Line
  - Literature Connection:
  - *The Story of Money* by Betsy Maestro — 56
- Lesson 10: Find Percents — 62
- Lesson 11: Picture Decimals — 64
- Lesson 12: The Ants' Picnic — 66
- Lesson 13: Get Off the Field! — 70
- Extensions and Homework — 72

5 • CAR BUYER'S PROJECT — 73

- Project Overview — 74
- Lesson 14: Car Buyer's Project • Phase I — 76
- Lesson 15: Car Buyer's Project • Phase II — 80
- Lesson 16: Graph Your Budget — 84
- Lesson 17: Car Buyer's Project • Phase III — 86
- Lesson 18: Student Self-Evaluation — 90

6 • THE STOCK MARKET PROJECT — 97

- Lesson 19: Track Toothpaste Stock
  - Literature Connection:
  - *The Toothpaste Millionaire* by Jean Merrill — 98
- Lesson 20: Graph Your Stock — 100
- Lesson 21: Did Your Stock Grow in Value? — 102

7 • WHAT DID WE LEARN? — 105

- Lesson 22: Mini-Portfolio—Assessment 3 — 106

TEACHER RESOURCES — 111

- Reproducible Pages — 112
- Bibliography — 133
- Index — 133

STUDENT ACTIVITY PAGES — 135

WELCOME TO MATHZONES

Welcome to the MathZones! We invite you to join the many teachers who are facilitating a new kind of learning in their classrooms. The lessons in this resource guide will help you create an exciting and supportive learning environment with your students.

Imagine your classroom. Students are on task, sharing ideas and strategies, and checking results before they hand in their papers. Imagine having the time to work with individuals and small groups of students. Imagine your feeling of success when your students demonstrate proficiency in many math concepts.

In this unit, students will learn to:

- represent the same numbers in fractions, decimals, and percents.
- apply this skill to interpreting stock market charts.
- relate use of decimals to working with money, including designing budgets.
- reason and communicate about math ideas as they relate to real-life situations.

Writing and talking about mathematics are integrated throughout to provide a powerful learning and teaching tool. Each activity integrates language arts objectives—speaking, listening, writing—as students talk about mathematics and write about their understanding and their solution strategies.

"Understanding multiple representations for numbers is a crucial precursor to solving many of the problems that students encounter. Toward this end, students can represent fractions, decimals, and percents in a variety of meaningful situations..."

NCTM Standards
pages 87

USING MATHZONES

Using This Unit	2
Using the Lesson Plan	4
Skills Matrix	6
Classroom Organization	8
Materials	9
Thinking and Talking Math	10
Four-Step Writing Plan	11
Using Math Journals	12
Teaching With Projects	13
Integrating Mathematics into the Curriculum	14
Teacher Talk	15
Family Involvement	16
Assessment	17

USING THIS UNIT

Using **Fractions, Decimals, and Percent** contains lessons that review and expand students' knowledge of place value, decimal points, and comparing and ordering decimals.

Assessments are open-ended and provide ongoing feedback about students' evolving understanding of fractions, decimals, and percent. The assessments in this unit are as follows:

Assessment 1: Write About Decimals
Students share prior knowledge and venture some generalizations about decimals.

Assessment 2: Estimate and Order Decimals
Students compare and order decimals.

Assessment 3: Mini-Portfolio
Students evaluate and revise their statements about decimals, fractions, and percentages.

For more information about **Assessment,** see page 17.

A **whole-group** learning activity begins most lessons. Whole-group instruction is usually followed by small, heterogeneous groups of students working together on another activity.
Cooperative learning or small-group instruction adds an exciting dimension to the learning of mathematics. Student benefits include:

- face-to-face interaction.
- group processing.
- individual accountability.
- increased self-esteem.
- development of social skills.
- higher-level thinking.
- increased individual achievement.

Four kinds of learning experiences are included in this unit:
- *Assessments*
- *Whole-group activities*
- *Cooperative-group activities*
- *Literature-based lessons*

Literature-based lessons in this unit suggest these books: ***The Story of Money*** by Betsy Maestro and ***The Toothpaste Millionaire*** by Jean Merrill. Additional titles are provided in the **Bibliography** starting on page 133.

In addition, this unit teaches students many useful skills and applications of decimals.

Students:
- read data from a chart; stock table.
- identify decimal place values.
- read and write decimals.
- compare and order decimals.
- subtract decimals.
- recognize the relationship between decimals and fractions
- balance a budget.
- use percent concepts.
- make a time line.
- apply rate formulas to determine stock values.

Unit Pacing

Using Fractions, Decimals, and Percent can be taught in six weeks as a free-standing math unit.

To help you plan the unit for your class, a **Skills Matrix** chart is provided on pages 6 and 7.

This unit suggests a sequence of teaching. However, we strongly suggest that you evaluate your students' needs and adjust the pacing of this unit and the selection of lessons to them.

USING THE LESSON PLAN

Lesson plans include:

- *Materials*
- *Advance Preparation*
- *Objectives*
- *Getting Started*
- *Wrapping Up*
- *Write About Math*
- *Teaching Tips*
- *Extension/ Homework*
- *What Really Happened*
- *Sharing Ideas and Strategies*

1 Each lesson is designed for easy planning and implementation. The first page of each lesson shows a list of **Materials.** It is conveniently placed in the margin for easy reference and lesson management. This list includes supplies that are required for both teachers and students.

2 **Advance Preparation** suggests ways teachers could prepare for the lesson and avoid any delays when introducing the lesson.

3 The second page of each lesson begins with a list of **Objectives**, clearly-written statements of what students will learn.

4 **Getting Started** launches the lesson. Ideas for warming up for the lesson are presented. Questions may be included to help students think critically and become independent learners. Guidelines for coaching students are often provided.

5 **Wrapping Up** offers ideas to close out a lesson. Sometimes a writing prompt suggestion is described under **Write About Math**. Students are encouraged to write in their math journals throughout the unit.

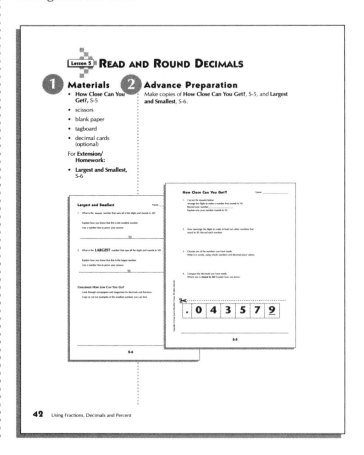

6 Teaching Tips offer advice on classroom management, questions to facilitate discussion, extension activities, or an informal assessment idea.

7 Extension/Homework activities are provided at the end of some lessons. In addition, the feature **Extensions and Homework** may appear at the end of a section. They relate to all lessons in the section.

8 What Really Happened provides vignettes from the classroom, sharing ways in which students transformed activities to meet their learning needs. These glimpses into one particular classroom are not intended to be prescriptive, but are provided as a way of sharing teaching and learning experiences.

9 Sharing Ideas and Strategies offer real-life student work—and comments that help interpret it as well as ideas for assessment.

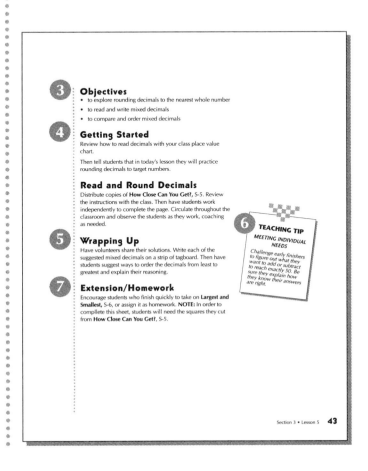

SKILLS MATRIX

Concepts and Skills	1. Write About Decimals—Assessment 1	2. Business Basics	3. Follow a Stock	4. Decimal Place Value Patterns	5. Read and Round Decimals	6. Read Decimals	7. Compare and Order Decimals	8. Estimate and Order Decimals—Assessment 2	9. Make a Time Line	10. Find Percents
Problem solving	✔	✔	✔	✔	✔	✔	✔	✔	✔	✔
Writing about math	✔	✔				✔	✔	✔		
Communication	✔	✔	✔	✔	✔	✔	✔	✔	✔	✔
Reasoning	✔	✔	✔	✔	✔	✔	✔	✔	✔	✔
Connections	✔	✔	✔	✔	✔	✔	✔	✔	✔	✔
Number relationship: see equivalents	✔			✔	✔					✔
Number relationships: apply ratio	✔			✔	✔	✔	✔	✔		✔
Number systems: develop and order whole numbers, fractions, and decimals	✔			✔	✔	✔	✔	✔	✔	
Computation				✔	✔					✔
Select appropriate method of computing										✔
Estimate, then compute, then check				✔				✔		✔
Describe patterns and functions	✔			✔	✔					✔
Analyze functional relationships	✔			✔	✔					✔
Solve equations				✔						
Collect, organize, and describe data		✔	✔						✔	
Construct and interpret graphs, charts		✔	✔						✔	
Statistics: make inferences based on data		✔								
Geometry: use geometric models				✔						✔
Measurement: choose proper units, scales									✔	
Compute or represent area or volume				✔						✔

	11. Picture Decimals	12. The Ants' Picnic	13. Get Off the Field!	14. Car Buyer's Project • Phase I	15. Car Buyer's Project • Phase II	16. Graph Your Budget	17. Car Buyer's Project • Phase III	18. Student Self-Evaluation	19. Track Toothpaste Stock	20. Graph Your Stock	21. Did Your Stock Grow in Value?	22. Mini-Portfolio—Assessment 3
	✓	✓	✓	✓	✓	✓	✓	✓	✓	✓	✓	✓
		✓				✓	✓			✓	✓	✓
	✓	✓	✓	✓	✓	✓	✓	✓	✓	✓	✓	✓
	✓	✓	✓	✓	✓	✓	✓	✓	✓	✓	✓	✓
	✓	✓	✓	✓	✓	✓	✓	✓	✓	✓	✓	✓
	✓					✓	✓			✓	✓	✓
	✓	✓	✓	✓		✓	✓	✓		✓	✓	
	✓	✓	✓	✓						✓	✓	✓
	✓	✓	✓	✓	✓	✓	✓	✓	✓	✓	✓	
	✓			✓	✓							
			✓	✓	✓							
										✓	✓	
										✓	✓	
	✓		✓	✓	✓	✓	✓	✓				
				✓	✓	✓	✓			✓	✓	
				✓	✓	✓			✓	✓		
						✓				✓	✓	
	✓	✓										
	✓	✓				✓				✓	✓	
	✓	✓										

CLASSROOM ORGANIZATION

Creating a Setting for Learning

There are many ways to organize a classroom for units such as this one. What follows is a description of how the classroom was organized as we taught this unit.

The philosophy in the classroom emphasized that we all learn from one another. Therefore, once an activity had been launched, students were asked to work in pairs or small groups. For the most part, they allowed to choose their partner or group. As activities came to closure, each pair or group presented their solution strategies. Classmates were encouraged to ask questions, compare strategies, and reconcile solutions.

Students tended to work with the same partner or group throughout the unit. This choice was acceptable as long as no one was feeling left out and the time together was spent focused on math.

MATERIALS

The activities in this unit emphasize hands-on learning. Most lessons refer to student activity pages, which are indicated by the prefix "S." For your convenience, we have provided reproducible **Student Activity Pages** at the back of the book. (See page 135 for an overview.) You will also find reproducible copymasters in the **Teacher Resources** section. These include centimeter graph paper, stock information, and more. See page 111 for an overview.

Advance Preparation ideas and reminders are provided on the **Materials** page for each lesson and often include reproducible student activity pages.

Classroom Materials

In addition to supplies listed on the **Materials** page, you will need the following classroom supplies:

- paper
- math journals
- pencils
- markers
- rulers
- scissors

Recommended Literature Library

The Story of Money by Betsy Maestro (New York: Clarion Books, 1993)

The Toothpaste Millionaire by Jean Merrill (Boston: Houghton Mifflin, 1972)

For more books about this unit, refer to the Bibliography starting on page 133.

THINKING AND TALKING MATH

Opportunities to talk and write about mathematics create a powerful teaching and learning tool. Throughout this unit, students are asked to explain, orally and in writing, their ideas about decimals, fractions, and percent.

Group discussions are a good place to start the process of reflecting about mathematics. By sharing their experiences as learners throughout the unit, students hear problem-solving strategies. They share their peers' difficulties or successes. They begin to recognize and label the strategies they can use.

Writing is a natural follow-up to these group discussions. You can take advantage of this natural flow by allowing time for writing in journals after the class discussion.

The NCTM **Standards** say that the study of mathematics should include opportunities to communicate so that students can model situations using oral, written, concrete, pictorial, graphical, and algebraic methods.

Students learn to model situations in this unit. In addition to talking and writing about math, students represent centuries on a time line, the movement of stock prices on a line graph, and a family budget on a pie graph.

They draw pictures of decimals and fractions, sometimes discovering they are drawing the same number! They learn to use models to visualize solutions, which they then represent algebraically. Drawings and models often find a place in their final communication about their solution to the problem.

FOUR-STEP WRITING PLAN

The four-step writing plan outlined below is a valuable learning tool that helps students develop their own problem-solving strategies. You can use these questions as discussion prompts or as writing prompts. This plan also provides questioning strategies that help you coach students to become powerful, independent problem solvers.

1. *What are you trying to find out?*
   Restate the problem in your own words.

   When students restate a problem, they are better able to understand what the problem is about. Restating a problem encourages students to make it their own. Restating a problem also encourages students to ask questions they may have about the situation and/or about the data.

2. *What are your first impressions?*
   How do you think you might solve this problem?

   Encouraging students to express their first impressions allows them to consider how this problem is like other problems they have encountered. Some students need to write about their anxieties before they can gain the courage to take on a challenge.

3. *How did you find your answer?*
   Describe your strategy so that someone else can try it.

   When students explain their strategies, they reflect on their thinking. Here you can assess for conceptual understandings and encourage students to develop a repertoire of problem-solving strategies that is meaningful to the student. Most importantly, when students explain their strategies, they come to value their own thinking.

4. *How do you know your answer is right?*
   Could there be more than one right answer? Why or why not?

   Encouraging students to examine their answers helps develop independent thinking. When students explain the reasonableness of their answers, they validate their methods and computational accuracy. As students explain how they know their answer is right, they learn to rely on themselves rather than on the approval of the teacher. When students discuss answers, they learn to develop listening skills; they build their own language skills; they learn to evaluate their own thinking.

USING MATH JOURNALS

Math journals help students keep a record of their thinking and of the evolution of their ideas. For each **Write About Math** prompt, we ask students to start on a clean page and clearly label the date and the topic.

We have tried various kinds of notebooks and find that steno pads work well. The pages are large enough to encourage students to "think in writing," yet are not so large that much paper is wasted. Steno pads are also relatively inexpensive and easy to find in bulk in office supply stores.

We have also had good experiences with spiral-bound graph paper notebooks. Graph paper helps organize writing and sketches. Equations can be aligned along a vertical line. Tables and charts can be easily set up on a grid. However, graph paper journals are relatively expensive.

When you consider what you will have your students use for math journals, you may want to keep in mind:

Size: A math journal need not have more than 32 pages. If your students are using student activity pages, you may prefer that they purchase a folder or spiral notebook to keep all related papers together in one place.

Cost: Will students supply their own journals or does your school budget allow for this purchase? Steno pads are relatively inexpensive.

Creative Alternatives: Does your school's supply room provide blue composition books? If these are available, have holes drilled so students can keep them in their binders.

Does your supply shelf contain construction paper, plain paper, or newsprint? If so, have students make their own 32-page journals by stapling or fastening together sheets of paper inserted into a sheet of construction paper that has been folded in half.

Whatever format you choose, encourage students to use their journals. Many of our lessons have a writing prompt or a problem for student journals. Journals can be helpful in showing student growth as the year progresses. If you use portfolio assessment, a journal can be an important component.

TEACHING WITH PROJECTS

Projects are one of the most powerful vehicles to engage upper elementary students in learning mathematics. Projects are for everyone, regardless of whether needed paper and pencil skills have been fully mastered. When you make projects a central part of your math curriculum, you help all students make connections between math skills and the applications of these skills in the real world. Finally, projects help you assess holistically your students' problem-solving strategies and skills. Projects should never be reserved only for enrichment.

Time for projects can be built into your math lesson when you concentrate skills development into short practice sessions. The **Mental Math Warm-Up** activities provide practice with mental math and reasoning skills in a number context. These teacher-directed activities help to focus students for math time. At the same time, these activities give students repeated opportunities to develop confidence with basic mental math skills in an engaging format. We have found that students who initially feel insecure with the given skill, develop confidence and mastery when they are given repeated opportunities to practice in this setting.

INTEGRATING MATHEMATICS INTO THE CURRICULUM

Using Fractions, Decimals, and Percent provides lessons that are connected to the real world.

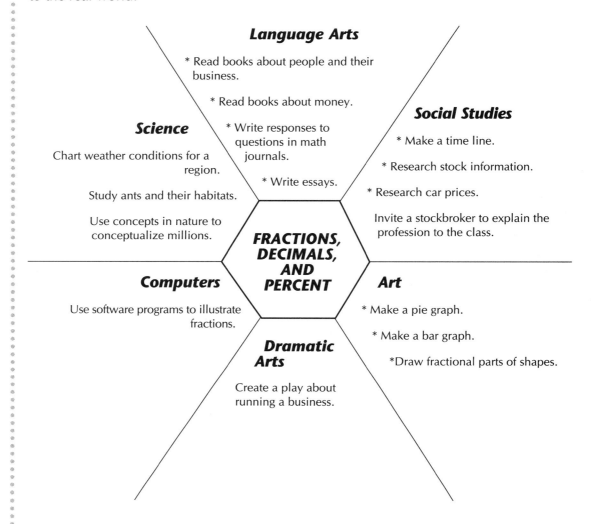

Language Arts
* Read books about people and their business.
* Read books about money.
* Write responses to questions in math journals.
* Write essays.

Social Studies
* Make a time line.
* Research stock information.
* Research car prices.
Invite a stockbroker to explain the profession to the class.

Science
Chart weather conditions for a region.
Study ants and their habitats.
Use concepts in nature to conceptualize millions.

Computers
Use software programs to illustrate fractions.

Dramatic Arts
Create a play about running a business.

Art
* Make a pie graph.
* Make a bar graph.
* Draw fractional parts of shapes.

FRACTIONS, DECIMALS, AND PERCENT

* Integrations included in this unit.

TEACHER TALK

Using Calculators

Calculators are not a replacement for basic pencil and paper arithmetic. At the same time, calculators are necessary tools that students must learn to use well. How do we reconcile the two demands—good mental math skills and technological expertise?

In this unit, calculators are an important problem-solving tool. We have found that students are better able to do exciting work with real-life applications of decimals, such as problems with money and investments, when they are not bogged down with tedious and lengthy computation. We have found that when students use calculators to supplement their emerging skills mastery, their involvement with math improves and they build the confidence needed to deal with the paper-and-pencil challenge. When we want students to exercise mental math skills, we assign a **Mental Math Warm-Up** activity that develops an awareness of number patterns and functional relationships through mental math.

FAMILY INVOLVEMENT

Today we are promoting teaching mathematics in a way substantially different from the way in which most of us were taught. The new pedagogy emphasizes problem solving over rote procedures, explanations of thought processes in addition to mere answers, and teamwork in the learning process rather than competition. The pedagogy endorsed by the National Council of Teachers of Mathematics *Curriculum and Evaluation Standards for School Mathematics* and other influential documents seeks to develop critical thinking as a habit of mind for all.

Building parental support for this way of teaching begins with acknowledging parents' concerns about the math instruction that seems foreign to their experience and their expectations. It is helpful when addressing parent concerns to begin by explaining the purposes of this unit, emphasizing the importance of allowing students time to make models so they discover certain truths for themselves.

This unit offers family members many opportunities to get involved. If you are fortunate to have volunteers in the classroom, ask them to help students track stocks in the paper. Parents whose careers involve business, finance, or stocks might share some real-world experiences with the class.

However, this unit also works fine if families cannot be involved. Most lessons are set up so that students progress by doing hands-on lessons. They also help each other learn.

Extensions and homework suggestions can be found throughout the unit.

ASSESSMENT

The goals of this unit go beyond the traditional test objectives. You will be able to assess for this knowledge informally throughout the unit as you observe your students' progress with computing percents for their car payments or converting stock prices from their newspaper reports to decimal format. (For example, students will learn that a share reported as $3^4/_8$ is worth $3.50.)

By the time students have reached the upper elementary grades, they have had experiences with fractions and decimals. However, many students have difficulty realizing that the same number can be represented in many different ways. They need practice in seeing that a fraction can be easily converted to a decimal.

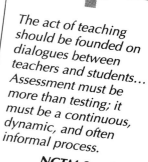

The act of teaching should be founded on dialogues between teachers and students... Assessment must be more than testing; it must be a continuous, dynamic, and often informal process.
NCTM Standards
page 203

The assessments built into this unit are designed to evaluate what students already know and how they use their prior knowledge to communicate about decimals. The assessments are designed to encourage students to use their observation skills and informal language to name and describe what they know about place value. The assessments are designed to support instruction and learning.

Assessment 1, **Write About Decimals**, invite students to think broadly about the topic and give teachers feedback about the class' standing point. Assessment 2, **Estimate and Order Decimals**, evaluates students' understanding of decimals. Assessment 3, **Mini-Portfolio**, helps students summarize their learning in a common written format and provides another form of closure.

Portfolio assessments provide a fourth evaluation tool. In this assessment students reflect on their learning as they assemble a collection of their favorite and notable projects. Portfolios are most successful when they are introduced at the beginning of the unit. Explain that you will be including a portfolio assessment and explain the scoring rubric at the beginning of the unit. Some teachers develop the rubric together with their students. Students (or you) will keep their assignments in a safe place for the duration of the unit. At the end, students will reflect on their work, write a letter explaining their choices for their portfolios, design a cover, rewrite a learning letter, and assemble their portfolios. **Car Buyer's Project • Self-Evaluation**, S-27, and **Car Buyer's Project • Grading Your Own Work**, S-28, allow students to evaluate their work and assign themselves grades. These pages can be placed in students' portfolios.

Whatever assessment tools you choose, be assured that you will measure much progress as your students learn about fractions, decimals, and percent.

WHAT DO YOU KNOW ABOUT DECIMALS?

SECTION 1

**LESSON 1: WRITE ABOUT DECIMALS—
ASSESSMENT 1** 20

Lesson 1: WRITE ABOUT DECIMALS

Materials
- **Write About Decimals,** S-1
- chart paper
- marker

Advance Preparation
Make a copy of **Write About Decimals**, S-1, for each student.

Name _____ Date _____

Write About Decimals

1. Think about what you already know about decimals. List your ideas on a separate sheet of paper. Then underline two ideas that you think are the most important.
   Explain why these ideas are important for understanding decimals.

2. How are decimals like money? How are they different from money?

3. How are decimals like fractions? How are they different from fractions? Give specific examples. Use pictures if you want.

S-1

Using Fractions, Decimals and Percent

Objective
- to assess students' prior knowledge of decimals

Getting Started
Tell students that during this unit they will be learning about how decimals, or very small numbers, work. Explain that to find out what they already know about decimals, you are going to ask the class a few questions.

Write About Decimals
Distribute copies of **Write About Decimals**, S-1. Ask students to answer each question as fully as they can.

Circulate and observe the students as they work. If they are having trouble getting started, prompt them by suggesting:

"What is one thing you know about decimals? (HINT: Think about how we write teeny tiny numbers or very big numbers.)"

"Now think about another thing you know about decimals and add that to your paragraph or list."

"Draw a picture that shows a decimal. Then write about your picture."

"Think about a time when you had to use decimals. Then describe the experience."

Allow up to twenty minutes for the writing. Then gather the class for discussion.

Wrapping Up
Ask students to share one thing they know about decimals. Make a list of ideas and record them on a chart. Include all ideas, even those that may seem wrong. Remind the class that they will have a chance to review and revise their ideas at the end of the unit.

Save the class chart; you will review it during closure of this unit.

What Really Happened

At first, students seemed to feel overwhelmed by the questions we asked. We saw many blank papers and wondered whether students knew so much already that it was hard to focus on a few ideas.

"Let's think about it this way," we suggested. "Write down just one thing that you happen to know about decimals—anything at all." This suggestion seemed to help everyone get started. Pretty soon, pages were filling up with ideas.

When a student seemed stumped, we suggested that he or she move on to one of the other questions. We reminded students that this was not a test but just a survey to help us understand what the class was ready to learn next.

Students demonstrated a range of prior knowledge of decimals as well as some interesting misconceptions. Most students had some idea that decimals were related to fractions because both concepts referred to parts of a number. Others knew that decimals had something to do with a dot and money, or with whole numbers and parts of numbers. A few students demonstrated that they had more experience with the mechanics of operating with decimals and fraction equivalents. It was clear that all students would benefit from further investigations.

The summary looked like this:

Important Things to Know About Decimals

1. Without a dot there is no decimal.
2. They're less than a whole.
3. A decimal is another way to show fractions.
4. Decimals separate the whole numbers from the fraction.
5. A decimal that has a dot is a really small number like the chart in our room that shows pi = 3.1415926535 . . . .
6. The decimal part is to the right of the dot.
7. Decimals show a fraction of a number.
8. Decimals are used in money and fractions.
9. Decimals are lots of little numbers that hardly count.
10. parts of a number
11. Value of the number gets smaller as you go to the right.
12. divides the dollars from the cents

Sharing Ideas and Strategies

Like several students in the class, Jane had had experiences with decimals. However, her understanding of decimal concepts is spotty. She will benefit from "talking decimals"—to hear the relationship between decimals and fractions.

> A decimal can explain a fraction of a number. Like 3.5 can stand for 3 and a half. And 3.10 can stand for a whole.
>
> You can't put the dot anywhere It has to be right after the first digit, Or it might be assumed to be something else.
>
> Decimals can be like money like 3.5 billion dollars. Stands for 3 and a half billion dollars.
>
> Decimals are sort of a fraction. It's another way of writing it.
>
> 3.10 three goes into ten 3 R1. It's the same way writing it but not ÷, sideways with a dot.
>
> 3.3   Decimal fraction   3/3   5.10   5/10

> 1. The decimals always seperats a number, and it's never put in a whole number it seperates a whole number into half of one or a third or one of them. The whole number is on the left and the other number is on the right of the decimal.
>
> 2. The way I think decimals are related to money is by the cents and dollars it seperates it. The way it's not money is you can only buy knowleage from it, but you can't buy Good's with it.
>
> 3. A decimal is like a fraction becacause you sometimes you use it in a fraction. The way they are different is because you don't allways use them in fractions.

Andre, left, thinks very practically about how decimals and money are different. He points out that money can be used to buy things but that it isn't possible to spend decimals. Whereas money is concrete, decimals are definitely abstract.

1. All decimals are smaller than one. Decimals can go on for infinity but they are still very small. These ideas are important because decimals might be mistaken for large numbers. The dot is the most important thing about a decimal without the dot there is no decimal.

2. Decimals are sort of like cents $20.17 is the same as 20.17. But they are different because there always have to be two digits in the cents place, in decimals there can be infinity numbers, or one. If you are working with money and get this answer $5.731 you will have to round it to $5.73 because there can be only two digits in the cents place, in decimals, you don't have to. In money you can't use this number $2.5. You'll have to change it to $2.50 this is the same thing because $2.5 = $2\frac{5}{10}$, $2.50 = $2\frac{50}{100}$. In decimals you can simplify.

3. All decimals are only fractions and fractions of 10, 100, 1,000... For example .5 = $\frac{5}{10}$ .51 = $\frac{51}{100}$ .512 = $\frac{512}{1000}$ ...

Julie, an articulate writer, demonstrates a thorough understanding of decimal concepts, including how decimals round and how they convert. Julie will be encouraged to broaden her understanding through extension activities.

LAUNCH THE STOCK MARKET PROJECT

SECTION 2

- **Project Overview** — 26
- **Lesson 2: Business Basics** — 28
- **Lesson 3: Follow a Stock** — 34

Project Overview

In the Stock Market Project, students will use their knowledge of fractions, decimals, and graphing to help make sense of the stock market. They will learn a bit about the free enterprise system as they:

- choose a stock to follow for five weeks from a list of Selected U.S. Stocks (pages 114–116).
- learn how to look up stock prices in the newspapers.
- read **The Toothpaste Millionaire**, a story about a boy who invents a cheaper tube of toothpaste.
- apply what they have learned about money to solve problems based on **The Toothpaste Millionaire**.
- create line graphs showing their stocks' performance over five weeks (Did the stock go up or down?).
- compute the value of shares of this stock over the five weeks.

The Stock Market Project is most powerfully taught when students track a stock for five weeks. We suggest that students choose a stock early in this decimals unit. Choosing a stock and learning to read stock tables can be completed in two class sessions. Then tracking the stock is a quick daily routine that will not take away math time.

After working with decimals and completing The Car Buyer's Project, spend a week on the Stock Market Project. Use the data collected through the course of the unit for the final graph.

Advance Preparation

Business pages from newspapers are needed to track stocks. Check the business pages of your local newspapers. Do they publish stock listings? If so, how complete are their listings? Consider your class. Do students' families subscribe to newspapers? Can you assign reading these pages for homework?

If you feel it would be better to check stock prices during school hours, try one of these strategies:

- Use the school library.
- Have volunteers bring in sections of the paper. Ideally, a classroom will have four or five papers to share.
- Ask your local newspaper or a local brokerage house to contribute papers for the duration of the stock project.

WEEK 1: LAUNCHING THE STOCK MARKET PROJECT

Lesson 2: Business Basics

Students learn about the stock market, including the Law of Supply and Demand. They suggest an idea for a business that would be successful and choose a stock from a list of selected stocks (pages 114–116).

Lesson 3: Follow a Stock

Students learn how to read a stock's price in the newspaper. They record the daily price on a data sheet.

WEEKS 2-5: ONGOING ACTIVITIES

Students look up and record their stock's closing price on their data sheet Tuesday through Friday. (Newspapers do not carry stock tables on Mondays because the markets are closed over the weekend.) Start at the end of Week 1; wrap up four weeks later.

The class reads **The Toothpaste Millionaire.** Start at the beginning of Week 3 and read two chapters per day. You may choose to read the book aloud to the class or to have students read independently.

WEEK 6: USING DATA FROM THE STOCK MARKET PROJECT

Tracking Toothpaste Stock

Students compute the value of stock from **The Toothpaste Millionaire.** They graph the results.

Graph Your Stock

Students create a line graph that shows their stock's daily closing price over four weeks.

Did Your Stock Grow in Value?

Students compute the value of an imaginary $1,000 investment in their stock. They evaluate their stocks as investments.

Lesson 2: BUSINESS BASICS

Materials

- copies of **Selected U.S. Stocks,** pages 114–116, one set per four students
- overhead transparency
- overhead projector
- chart paper and markers

Advance Preparation

Make a transparency of one page from **Selected U.S. Stocks,** pages 114–116. Make copies of all three pages for students to share.

Start a class stock chart that students will fill out.

CLASS STOCK CHART			
Student Investor	Company	Abbreviation	Where

SELECTED U.S. STOCKS–1

Company Name	Address	Ticker Symbol/ WSJ Abbrev.	Where*
Apparel			
Gap Inc.	1 Harrison St., San Francisco, CA 94105-1602	GPS/Gap S	NYSE
Levi Strauss Assoc. Inc.	1155 Battery St., San Francisco, CA 94111-1256		NYSE
Oshkosh B'Gosh Inc.	112 Otter Ave., Oshkosh, WI 54901-5067	GOSHA/OshBA	NASDAQ
Ross Stores Inc.	8333 Central Ave., Newark, CA 94560-3440	ROST/RossStr	NASDAQ
Athletic Shoes			
L.A. Gear Inc.	2850 Ocean Park Blvd., Santa Monica, CA 90405-2936	LA/LA Gear	NYSE
Nike Inc.	1 SW Bowerman Dr., Beaverton, OR 97005-6453	NKE/NikeB	NYSE
Reebok International Ltd.	100 Technology Center Dr., Stoughton, MA 02072-4702	RBK/Reebok	NYSE
Biotechnology and Medical Products			
Coherent Inc.	5100 Patrick Henry Dr., Santa Clara, CA 95054-1112	COHR/Coherent	NASDAQ
Genentech	460 Point San Bruno Blvd., So.San Francisco, CA 94080-4990	GNE/Genentec	NYSE
Nellcor Inc.	4280 Hacienda Dr., Pleasanton, CA 94588-2719	Nell/Nellcor	NASDAQ
Comics and Cards			
Marvel Entertainment Grp.	387 Park Ave. S, 12th Fl., New York, NY 10016-8810	MRV/Marvel	NYSE
Score Board Inc.	1951 Old Cuthbert Rd., Cherry Hill, NJ 08034-1417	BSBL/ScoreBd	NASDAQ
Communications			
AirTouch Communications Corp.	425 Market St., 36th Fl., San Francisco, CA 94104-2406	ATI/AirTouch	NYSE
AT &T Corp.	32 Ave. of the Americas, New York, NY 10013-2473	T/AT&T	NYSE
MCI Communications Corp.	1801 Pennsylvania Ave. NW, Washington, DC 20006-3606	MCI/MCI	NASDAQ
Sprint Corp.	2330 Shawnee Mission Pkwy., Shawnee Mission, KS 66205-2005	FON/Sprint	NYSE
Computers and Software			
Adobe Systems Inc.	1585 Charleston Rd., Mtn. View, CA 94043-1225	ADBE/AdobeSy	NASDAQ
Apple Computer Inc.	20525 Mariani Ave., Cupertino, CA 95014-6202	AAPL/AppleC	NASDAQ
Broderbund Software Inc.	500 Redwood Blvd., Novato, CA 94947-6921	BROD/BrodSft	NASDAQ
Compaq Computer Corp.	20555 Sh 249, Houston, TX 77070	CPQ/Compaq	NYSE
Dell Computer Corp.	9505 Arboretum Blvd., Austin, TX 78759-7299	DELL/DellCpt	NASDAQ
Hewlett-Packard Co.	3000 Hanover St., Palo Alto, CA 94304-1181	HWP/HewlPk	NYSE
International Business Machines Corp.(IBM)	Old Orchard Rd., Armonk, NY 10504	IBM/IBM	NYSE
Intuit Inc.	66 Willow Place, Menlo Park, CA 94025-3601	INTU/Intuit	NASDAQ
Microsoft Corp.	1 Microsoft Way, Redmond, WA 98052-8300	MSFT/Microsoft	NASDAQ
Xerox Corp.	800 Long Ridge Rd., Stamford, CT 06902-1227	XRX/Xerox s	NYSE

*Key to Stock Exchanges or Markets (where stock is listed)
- NYSE — New York Stock Exchange
- AMEX — American Stock Exchange
- NASDAQ — National Association of Security Dealers Automated Quotation System

114 Using Fractions, Decimals and Percent

SELECTED U.S. STOCKS

Company Name	Address
Electronics	
Circuit City Stores Inc.	9950 Maryland Dr., Richmond, VA
Eastman Kodak Co. Inc.	343 State St., Rochester, NY 1465
Gametek	2999 NE 191st St., Ste 500, Miam
Food Products	
Campbell Soup	Campbell Place, Camden, NJ 0810
Chiquita Brands Intl. Inc.	250 E. 5th St., Cincinnati, OH 4520
Coca Cola Co. Inc.	1 Coca Cola Plaza NW, Atlanta, GA
Dole Food Co. Inc.	31355 Oak Crest Dr., Thousand Oa
Hershey Foods Corp.	100 Crystal A Drive, Hershey, PA 1
Kellogg Co.	1 Kellogg Square, Battle Creek, MI
Pepsico Inc.	Anderson Hill Rd., Purchase, NY 1
Quaker Oats Co. Inc.	321 N. Clark St., Chicago, IL 6061
RJR Nabisco Holdings Corp.	1301 Ave. of the Americas, New Y
Sara Lee Corp.	3-1st National Place, Chicago, IL 6
Smucker JM Co., The	Strawberry Lane, Orrville, OH 4466
Tootsie Roll Industries Inc.	7401 S. Cicero Ave., Chicago, IL 6
Wrigley Wm. Jr. Co. Inc.	410 N. Michigan Ave., Chicago, IL
Food Servers	
El Chico Restaurants Inc.	12200 N. Stemmons Fwy., Dallas,
IHOP Corp.	525 N. Brand Blvd., Glendale, CA
McDonald's Corp.	McDonald's Plaza, Hinsdale, IL 60
Showbiz Pizza Time Inc.	4441 W. Airport Fwy, Irving, TX 75
Sizzler Intl. Inc.	12655 W. Jefferson Blvd., Los Ang
TCBY Enterprises Inc.	425 W. Capitol Ave., Little Rock, A
Wendy's Intl. Inc.	4288 W. Dublin Granville Rd., Dub
Retailers/Wholesalers	
JCPenney Co. Inc.	6501 Legacy Dr., Plano, TX 75024
KMart Corp.	3100 W. Big Beaver Rd., Troy, MI
Natural Wonders Inc.	4299 Technology Dr., Fremont, CA
Price/Costco	10809 120th Ave. NE, Kirkland, W
Sears Roebuck & Co.	Sears Tower, Chicago, IL 60606
Toys "R" Us Inc.	461 From Rd., Paramus, NJ 07652
WalMart Stores	705 SW 8th St., Bentonville, AR 72

*Key to Stock Exchanges or Markets (where stock is listed)
- NYSE — New York Stock Exchange
- AMEX — American Stock Exchange
- NASDAQ — National Association of Security

SELECTED U.S. STOCKS

Company Name	Address
Services & Transportation	
Alaska Air Group Inc.	19300 Pacific Hwy. S., Seattle, WA
American Express Co. Inc.	200 Vesey St., American Express Tower, New Yor
Continental Airlines Inc.	2929 Allen Pky., Ste. 1100, Houste
Delta Air Lines Inc.	Hartsfield Intl. Airport, Atlanta, GA
Federal Express Corp.	2005 Corporate Ave., Memphis, T
Hilton Hotels Corp.	9336 Civic Center Dr., Beverly Hill
Sports/Outdoor Recreation	
Coleman Co. Inc.	250 N. St. Francis St., Wichita, KS
Gymboree Corp.	700 Airport Blvd., Ste 200, Burling
Harley-Davidson Inc.	3700 W. Juneau Ave., Milwaukee,
Huffy Corp.	7701 Byers Rd., Miamisburg, OH
Rawlings Sporting Goods Co. Inc.	1859 Intertech Pl., Fenton, MO 63
Toy Manufacturers	
Galoob Lewis Toys Inc.	500 Forbes Blvd., So. San Francisc
Hasbro Inc.	1027 Newport Ave., Pawtucket, RI
Mattel Inc.	333 Continental Blvd., El Segundo,
Tyco Toys Inc.	6000 Midlantic Dr., Mount Laurel,
TV/Movies	
CBS Inc.	51 W. 52nd St., New York, NY 100
Disney (Walt) Co. Inc.	500 S. Buena Vista St., Burbank, C
Time-Warner Inc.	75 Rockefeller Plaza, New York, N
Twentieth Century Fox Inc.	10201 W. Pico Blvd, Los Angeles,
Miscellaneous	
Exxon Corp.	225 Lyndon B. Johnson Fwy, Irvin
Ford Motor Co.	American Rd., Dearborn, MI 4812
General Motors Corp.	3044 W. Grand Blvd., Detroit, MI 4
Lockheed Martin	4500 Park Granada, Calabasas, CA

NOTE: Each newspaper uses its own abbreviat be able to recognize and identify their stock lis symbol and the *Wall Street Journal* abbreviation students update as needed.

*Key to Stock Exchanges or Markets (where s
- NYSE — New York Stock Exchange
- AMEX — American Stock Exchange
- NASDAQ — National Association of Securi

116 Using Fractions, Decimals and Percent

28 Using Fractions, Decimals and Percent

Objectives

- to consider products according to the Law of Supply and Demand
- to read data from a chart

Getting Started

Introduce the students to the key stock market concepts as explained on page 30.

Discuss the Law of Supply and Demand as suggested on page 30. Ask students for ideas on what types of products they think might be in demand.

Look at Some Companies

Display a page from **Selected U.S. Stocks** on the overhead. Discuss the types of companies that are listed. Find one sample company, and go over its name, address, ticker symbol/Wall Street Journal abbreviation, and where it is listed. Be sure students understand the difference between NYSE (the New York Stock Exchange) and NASDAQ.

Choose a Stock to Follow

Make available copies of **Selected U. S. Stocks** or copies of the business section of your local newspaper. Have students pick one stock to follow. After they have chosen a stock, have them write their names and stocks on the class chart. (If students wish to do extra research, they may choose other stocks not on this list.)

Wrapping Up

Post a class stock chart listing the name of each student's stock. As students pick a stock, have them write in the name of the company, its initials, and where it is traded.

Write About Math: Have students write to this prompt: *If you could start a business, what would it be? Why would there be a demand for your product?*

TEACHING TIP

CLASSROOM MANAGEMENT

When students write their names on the class stock chart, they are making a public commitment to their project. This helps involve them in the project.

Introduce the Stock Market

The first day you discuss the stock market, teach a few key concepts:

- Stock is a small piece of a company. You buy shares of stock.
- Companies sell stock to raise money to develop new inventions or products, to build new factories, or for other improvements.
- Anyone can buy stock shares in a publicly traded company. The price is determined by the Law of Supply and Demand. (If there are more buyers than sellers, the price will go up.)
- Most people want to buy stock in companies that are doing well so their stock prices will go up. Then, if they like, they can sell the stock at a profit. Other investors look for income; stocks will pay dividends (portions of the company's profit) each year to people who own their stocks.
- Companies are traded in different U.S. markets. Three major markets:
  NYSE (the New York Stock Exchange)
  the American Exchange
  NASDAQ (National Association of Securities Dealers Automated Quotation System)
- Many countries have stock markets. The stock market has been part of the United States for most of its history.

The Law of Supply and Demand

This is a key concept to introduce to students as they start to study the stock market. The Law of Supply and Demand determines the prices of products as well as the prices of stocks. You might teach it by saying:

> "Pretend it is a very hot summer day. A few lucky people have air conditioners and swimming pools, but most people are very hot. Stores are rapidly being emptied of their electric fans. What is going to happen to the price of the remaining fans if the store owner can set any price he wants?" (Students might guess that the price will go up. It is unlikely that the store manager will put them on sale, because the supply is so low.)

> "Now pretend you are at a food market. Tomatoes are in season—even your neighbors are giving them away. Will the food seller charge high prices for tomatoes today?" (Because the supply is plentiful, and tomatoes have a short shelf life, the price of tomatoes should drop.)

Then ask students how the Law of Supply and Demand might affect :

- prices of tickets to a very popular rock concert
- prices of shares of stock in a stock market
- the price of soda during the winter
- the price of winter coats in the spring

A Brief History of Stock Markets

In 1792, traders met under the buttonwood tree on Wall Street in the small city of New York. They were buying and selling bonds to pay for the Revolutionary War. Eventually, the first New York Stock Exchange moved indoors near the buttonwood tree.

Soon most cities had stock exchanges, but the New York Stock Exchange became the biggest in the land. New enterprises such as railroads, canals, and businesses sold shares of their stock to the public there.

Over 100 years ago, Alexander Graham Bell needed funds to manufacture his new invention, the telephone. Banks would not give him money, so he offered stock for sale. Investors who bought shares of his stock became very rich.

New technology has enabled the stock market to handle many more transactions each day. During the late 1800s, the telegraph and the electric stock ticker allowed people far from New York to buy and sell stocks there. Stockbrokers in New York did their trading for them.

Stocks are generally known by their initials, such as IBM and AT&T, or by other short names. Back in the days of ticker tapes, these abbreviations fit on the tape that came out of the ticker machine telling the price of stocks.

Computers now handle stock transactions. In 1971, a new computer network called NASDAQ was started. It doesn't have a market floor in New York but it handles nearly as much business as the New York Stock Exchange. In the United States, the American Exchange is the third big exchange.

Sometimes the prices of many stocks will drop at once. The Stock Market Crash of 1929 signaled the start of the Depression of the 1930s. In 1987, many stocks dropped at once, triggering a recession, and in the mid–1990s stock prices reached an all-time high. No one knows when, or if, the market will drop.

A MINI-GLOSSARY OF STOCK TERMS

Annual report - a report created by a company for its shareholders

The "Dow" - short for the Dow Jones Industrial Average, a daily average of 30 representative stocks from the New York Stock Exchange. When the prices of their shares rise, the Dow goes up. When their shares fall in value, the Dow goes down.

NASDAQ - a newer marketplace for stocks, often used by up-and-coming companies. Trades are done using computers. Stands for National Association of Securities Dealers Automated Quotation system.

New York Stock Exchange - where the largest corporations trade their stock. Also called NYSE or "The Big Board".

Prospectus - a publication describing sale of stock to the public

Stock - a small piece of a company that can be purchased. You can buy shares of stock in a company.

Stockbrokers - salespeople who are licensed to buy and sell shares of stock for other people

Stockholders or shareholders - people who own stock

Stock market - where people buy and sell shares of stock

What Really Happened

Some students saw potential in creating a business using new ideas and new technology.

> I would make a computer company because lots of people are buying computers now. There are no computers that are very easy to work with so I'd make a company that makes computers that are easy to set up and easy to put programs on.

Marc (top) and David (right) suggested new developments for computers.

> **Micro Tech**
> My company will make a long line of hand held computers. Computers with big buttons for the elderly. Friendly, big talking computers for babies.

> A Medicine Company, because Medicine is in great demand. I would not only make regular medicines, like cold medicine, I would be a scientist who creates medicines and cures for major deseases. My company would also own a couple clinics, to cure people of deseases that cant be cured with medicine. My company would be called Cure & Co.

Julie (left) suggested developing new drugs for a profitable company.

> **The Capture Gun** — Wepons for the police
> A gun that fires a liqued plastic ballon that wraps around the enemy and feeds them air but doesn't kill them. The enemy falls to the ground and stays there untill you get there.

Glen (left) suggested a new tool for law-enforcement.

> I would start a chair company. I think it would be very successful because everybody sits in chairs.

> I would go with clothes because thousands of people buy them daily. They are also a necessitie of life!!!

> ## My Business
> My business would be a grocery called Health Hill. It would be a health store. The products sold there would be crushed ice fruit drinks, healthy sweets, granola, and other basic lowfat groceries, such as fresh fruits.
> Our locations would be in San Francisco, Los Angeles, New York, Woodside, Denver, Boston, London, Paris, Hong Kong, Tahitti, Hawaii, Kansas City, and Atherton. We would excell in selling Yogurt smoothies.
> Here is our logo:
>
>
>
> Here is our slogan:
> "Help yourself. Climb Health Hill."

Other students chose businesses that supply life's necessities so the demand will remain constant.

Louise pointed out the need for chairs, while Sonya made a case for a clothes company. Chrissy came up with a healthful fast food concept.

Lesson 3 — FOLLOW A STOCK

Materials

- overhead transparency
- overhead projector
- business section of the newspaper (one copy for each pair of students)
- **Stock Table Sleuths,** S-2
- **Stock Recording Sheet,** S-3
- rulers
- calculators

Advance Preparation

Provide for student access to newspapers as described on page 35. Study your newspaper's stock listing pages so you can locate the NYSE, AMEX, and NASDAQ listings.

Make a transparency of **Stock Table Sleuths,** S-2.

Make a copy of **Stock Recording Sheet,** S-3, for each student.

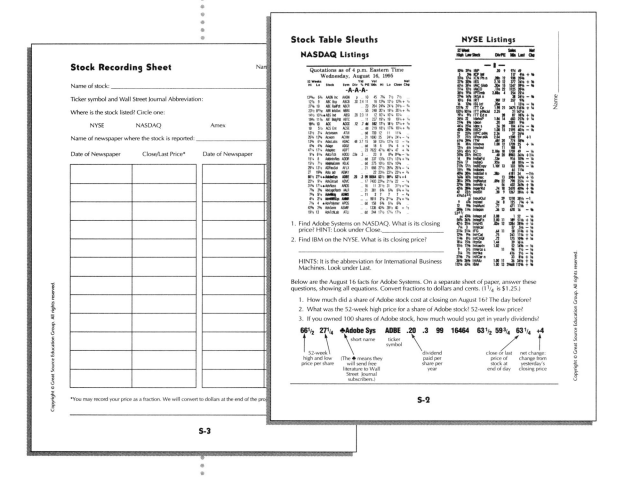

34 Using Fractions, Decimals and Percent

Objective
- to read data from a stock table

Getting Started
Display your prepared transparency of S-2. Describe how to interpret the key information (in this case, the closing price) in a stock table. Emphasize what students must know to look up the closing price of a stock:

- where it is traded (NYSE? NASDAQ? AMEX?)
- its initials or short name

Have students work on **Stock Table Sleuths,** S-2. Then tell students that they will begin tracking the performance of their personal stock using real newspapers. Point out that they will get into the habit of looking up their stock's closing price on Tuesday through Friday for the next five weeks and that after tracking the stock for a month, they will use their stock data to make a line graph showing movement of the stock.

Follow a Stock
Distribute newspapers and other materials. Have students share business sections and help each other locate their stocks. Show how using a ruler can help to read just one row of data. When students first get started, you may find that you need to help them remember on which exchange their stock is traded. Have them refer to the class chart that you have posted. If students cannot locate their first choice of stock in available newspaper listings, let them choose another stock.

Students will record personal stock data on **Stock Recording Sheet,** S-3. They will add to this sheet daily for four weeks. Circulate, observe, and coach as needed.

Wrapping Up
Have students share their results. Ask: "Whose stocks are listed on the New York Stock Exchange? the American Stock Exchange? NASDAQ?" Make a bar graph of the results.

Compare closing prices. After you have a sample of five students' prices, ask: "If you had $1,000 to invest, how many shares could you buy of each of these stocks?" Have students estimate using mental math; then have them figure out the answers on a calculator.

TEACHING TIP
USING LOGICAL REASONING
Explain to students that companies are listed alphabetically by their full names, not their company abbreviations. For example, IBM is alphabetized under international (International Business Machines).

TEACHING TIP
REACHING ALL LEARNERS
Students need to learn how to analyze data in a chart. Most charts display more data than is needed for a research task. It is important for students to sort the data and to focus only on the data they need. Explain that it is OK to ignore the other data at this time.

TEACHING TIP

MEETING INDIVIDUAL NEEDS

If students are not keeping up with tracking their stock, they may be having trouble locating a newspaper or using the stock table.

Bring in a paper daily and help students use the tables.

Practice with a supportive coach will build competence.

What Really Happened

We have used this unit for several years and offer these suggestions to help your stock market project go smoothly.

1. Have students look up their closing prices every weekday from Tuesday through Friday. Practice makes this easier. The class that tried looking up prices just once a week never got enough practice to have it go smoothly.

2. Make sure students write key abbreviations and information about exchanges on their recording sheets. The main cause of student confusion was not knowing where the stock was traded.

3. Keep track of student recording sheets. If students track their stocks daily in class you may find it helpful to keep all recording sheets in the classroom. If you have students track their stocks for homework, plan to check each day to see that their recording sheets are up-to-date.

4. Use the charts provided on pages 114–116. They were created to simplify researching stocks, their abbreviations, and where they are traded.

5. If possible, assign stock data recording as homework. If students have trouble keeping track of homework, have them take notes at home and transfer their data to the sheets filed away at school.

6. Keep a clearly labeled library of back issues of stock listing pages. Write the date in marker on the top of the page. This resource can help students fill in gaps in their data.

7. Daily newspaper delivery is essential if you plan to do this project only at school. Get families and businesses involved. Paid subscriptions might be worthwhile for a month.

DECIMAL CONCEPTS

SECTION 3

- **Lesson 4: Decimal Place Value Patterns** — 38
- **Lesson 5: Read and Round Decimals** — 42
- **Lesson 6: Read Decimals** — 46
- **Lesson 7: Compare and Order Decimals** — 48
- **Lesson 8: Estimate and Order Decimals— Assessment 2** — 50

Lesson 4: DECIMAL PLACE VALUE PATTERNS

Materials
- **Place Value Patterns, S-4**
- overhead transparency
- overhead projector
- calculators

Advance Preparation
Make a transparency of S-4 to display on an overhead projector.

Make a copy of S-4 for each student.

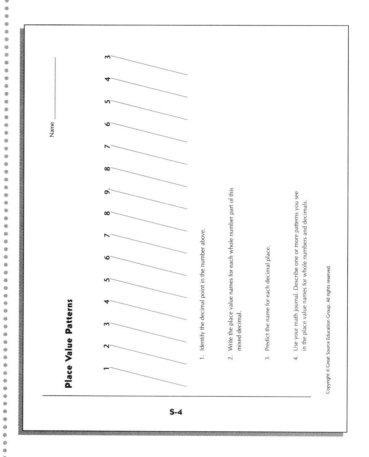

38   Using Fractions, Decimals and Percent

Objectives
- to review whole-number place value through millions
- to find patterns in whole-number and decimal place value
- to identify decimal place values through millionths

Getting Started
Display the transparency of S-4 using an overhead projector. Ask students what they notice about the number presented. Students should recognize that this number is a mixed decimal because it has a whole-number part and a decimal part. Explain that students will review whole-number place values and then look for patterns that help predict decimal place values.

Decimal Place Value Patterns
Distribute copies of **Place Value Patterns,** S-4, and explain that this is a reference sheet. Have students name the whole-number place values they know, beginning from the decimal point, and write them on the lines provided.

Then ask, "What number do I multiply by to get from the ones place to the tens place?" (10) Let students experiment using calculators. Then ask, "What do I multiply by to get from the tens place to the hundreds place?" (10) Continue in the same way through the millions place. Ask students what patterns they notice. Students should recognize that each place value is ten times greater than the previous place. Then ask, "What do I divide by to get from hundred-thousands to ten-thousands?" (10) "What do I divide by to get from ten-thousands to thousands?" (10)

Tell students that they will apply this pattern to identify decimal place values. Ask, "What do I get if I divide 1 by 10?" (One-tenth) "What do we call the first place to the right of the decimal point?" (Tenths) Draw a loop to connect the tens place and the tenths place. Then ask students to use this pattern to predict the names of the next four decimal places.

Wrapping Up
Have students finish S-4. Then invite them to share their place value predictions and explain their reasoning.

What Really Happened

Students felt that they were in familiar territory with this activity and happily went on autopilot. A surprising number filled in the whole number place values incorrectly, as in the example on the right.

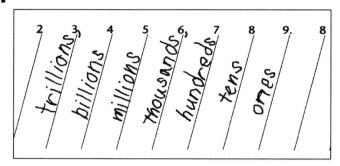

We decided to make a class chart. We reviewed period names (ones, thousands, millions) and the pattern within each period of ones, tens, hundreds to name place values. Then we gave students time to correct their place value charts.

To help students visualize the place value patterns as a system of multiplying by tens, we set out a display of base-ten materials. We discussed the math behind each piece.

How many of these tiny cubes will make a rod?
What multiplication equation can we write?
   (1 × 10)

How many of these rods make a flat? (10)
How many of these units make a flat? (100)
What multiplication equations can we write for units to rods to flats?
   (100 = 1 × 10 × 10)

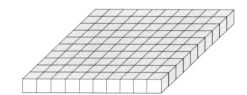

How many of these flats make a big cube? (10)
What multiplication equations can we write for units to rods to flats to big cube?
   (1,000 = 1 × 10 × 10 × 10)

What would a stack of 10 big cubes look like?
   (a giant rod)

How many tiny cubes would fit into that stack?
   (10,000)

What multiplication equation can we write for units to rods to flats to big cube to giant rod?
   (10,000 = 1 × 10 × 10 × 10 × 10)

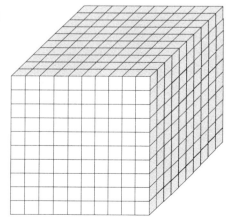

Most students understood that to get from the tens place to the thousands place they had to multiply by 100 (10 x 10). A few students, however, suggested multiplying by 20 (since two tens = 20). We suggested that they test their predictions using calculators. Experimenting with calculators was an effective strategy for many students to develop an awareness of patterns in our place value system.

Working out a mathematical rule for getting from millions to hundred-thousands was not obvious for some students even though they knew that division "undoes" multiplication. Verbally emphasizing the key numbers (as presented in boldface in the questions below) helped some students visualize the process.

"Picture this situation. If I had ten-thousand dollars to distribute to ten students, how much money would each student get?" (1,000)

"Now picture this. If I had a dollar to share among ten students, **what fraction of a dollar** would each student get? What equation could we write to show what we did to share the dollar?"

"How many **hundred-thousands** can you take out of one **million**?"

"Think about a pattern. If we can multiply ten-thousand by ten to get a hundred-thousand, what would we divide a hundred-thousand by to get ten-thousand?" (10, because of inverse operations)

We reviewed the multiplication and division patterns again after filling in the complete chart to reinforce the idea that there are mathematical rules (multiplying or dividing by 10) that let us move through the place value system.

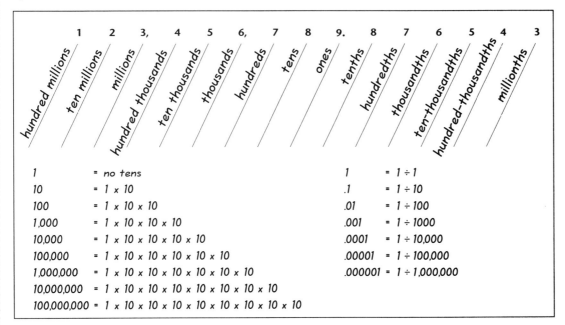

Our class chart looked like this. It was a valuable resource as students worked through this unit.

Lesson 5: Read and Round Decimals

Materials
- **How Close Can You Get?**, S-5
- scissors
- blank paper
- tagboard
- decimal cards (optional)

For **Extension/Homework:**
- **Largest and Smallest**, S-6

Advance Preparation
Make copies of **How Close Can You Get?**, S-5, and **Largest and Smallest**, S-6.

Largest and Smallest   Name _____

1. What is the SMALLEST number that uses all of the digits and rounds to 50?

   Explain how you know that this is the smallest number.
   Use a number line to prove your answer.
   _____ 50

2. What is the LARGEST number that uses all the digits and rounds to 50?

   Explain how you know that this is the largest number.
   Use a number line to prove your answer.
   _____ 50

CHALLENGE: HOW LOW CAN YOU GO?
Look through newspapers and magazines for decimals and fractions.
Copy or cut out examples of the smallest numbers you can find.

S-6

How Close Can You Get?   Name _____

1. Cut out the squares below.
   Arrange the digits to make a number that rounds to 50.
   Record your number _____.
   Explain why your number rounds to 50.

2. Now rearrange the digits to make at least two other numbers that round to 50. Record each number.

3. Choose one of the numbers you have made.
   Write it in words, using whole numbers and decimal place values.

4. Compare the decimals you have made.
   Which one is **closest to 50**? Explain how you know.

✂------------------------------------

| . | 0 | 4 | 3 | 5 | 7 | 9 |

S-5

---

42   Using Fractions, Decimals and Percent

Objectives
- to explore rounding decimals to the nearest whole number
- to read and write mixed decimals
- to compare and order mixed decimals

Getting Started
Review how to read decimals with your class place value chart.

Then tell students that in today's lesson they will practice rounding decimals to target numbers.

Read and Round Decimals
Distribute copies of **How Close Can You Get?**, S-5. Review the instructions with the class. Then have students work independently to complete the page. Circulate throughout the classroom and observe the students as they work, coaching as needed.

Wrapping Up
Have volunteers share their solutions. Write each of the suggested mixed decimals on a strip of tagboard. Then have students suggest ways to order the decimals from least to greatest and explain their reasoning.

Extension/Homework
Encourage students who finish quickly to take on **Largest and Smallest,** S-6, or assign it as homework. **NOTE:** In order to complete this sheet, students will need the squares they cut from **How Close Can You Get?**, S-5.

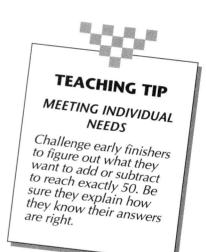

TEACHING TIP

MEETING INDIVIDUAL NEEDS

Challenge early finishers to figure out what they want to add or subtract to reach exactly 50. Be sure they explain how they know their answers are right.

What Really Happened

Most students had plenty of ideas for numbers that would round to 50. However, a few students seemed stumped. A conversation with one group of students went like this:

> "We don't get it," Nick, Janaina, and Josefina said.
>
> "Well, give me a number that is close to 50," I said. The group suggested 40 and 60.
>
> "Great. Now give me a number that is closer to 50 than 40," I suggested next.
>
> "47," Nick volunteered.
>
> "Can you get even closer?" I asked.
>
> "49," Janaina offered.
>
> "Good. Now let's get even closer," I prodded. The group hesitated, perplexed.
>
> "51. Nah, that's no closer than 49. There aren't any," they concluded.
>
> "Are there any numbers between 49 and 50?" I asked next.
>
> "Oh, yeah! 49 and a half," Janaina said.
>
> "Nick, can you get closer than that?" I asked.
>
> "How about 49 and three quarters." Nick ventured.
>
> "Great! Can you get even closer than that?" Josefina had been arranging her number tiles. She made 49.0357 and was ready to share her idea. "That's an interesting number," I responded. "That is a decimal that rounds to 49."
>
> "No, it rounds to 50, because that's the nearest ten," Janaina defended Josefina's idea.
>
> "That's true," I answered. "But you can make a decimal that is even closer to 50 if you are rounding to the nearest one."
>
> "You mean, like right here next to the point?" Janaina asked next, pointing to Josefina's model.
>
> "Oh! I get it! You have to get past point 5." Josefina made 49.7530.

These students were stumped because their most vivid experiences with rounding involved rounding to tens and hundreds. They were also still building their confidence about decimals. Once they focused on the digits in the decimal places, they were able to find many numbers that rounded to 50.

Jeremy was one of several students who believed that only numbers less than 50 could be correct solutions.

Class discussion was a valuable way to expand these students' understanding and informally introduce the idea of absolute value.

> First I didn't understand it but when I did it was easy. 49.7530 I did the one. I was trying to get the same thing for each lowest 49.7503 to get the highest not the so I stayed in the same area.
> ~~49.7305~~
> I couln't use fifty because after the decimal it already over
> Forty-nine sevendy-three hundreths and five tenthousandths

Using Fractions, Decimals and Percent

Sharing Ideas and Strategies

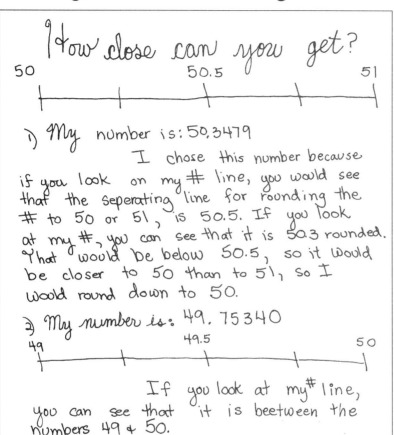

At first, Lauren was sure that 50.753 was correct, but she did not know how to prove it. We suggested that she draw a number line to test her idea. By placing benchmarks on a number line that showed mixed fractions between 50 and 51, Lauren discovered that her suggested mixed decimal was actually closer to 51 than 50. Like many students, Lauren corrected her guesswork by explaining her reasoning through a visual model.

50.475

Several students wanted to know how to decide what the significant rounding number is when a string of digits lay in the decimals places. For example, one student had formed 50.475 and wanted to know if the 7 rounds to 8 because the 5 rounds up, and if the 4 rounds up to 5, and the whole number then rounds to 51. We suggested that he think about the entire decimal part of his number and read it aloud. When he heard himself say "four hundred seventy-five thousandths" he realized that that fraction is less than half, so his number actually rounds down to 50.

TEACHING TIP

REACHING ALL LEARNERS

Encourage students to read the decimal parts aloud and hear their words.

This may help them visualize the decimal part of the number more clearly.

Section 3 • Lesson 5

Lesson 6: READ DECIMALS

Materials
- 4"x 6" index cards or tagboard
- marker
- overhead grid paper transparency
- overhead projector

Advance Preparation
Use tagboard to make several sets of digit cards (0 through 9) and one large decimal point card.

This game can be combined with **Compare and Order Decimals** (pages 48–49).

Objectives
- to write and read decimal numbers
- to explore the meaning of zeroes in decimals

Getting Started

Explain that students will play "Follow the Bouncing Decimal Point" to practice forming, reading, comparing, and ordering decimals. Plan to play this game as a warm-up for the next five days.

Read Decimals

Divide the class into teams of six students. Give each team a set of digit cards. Students select one digit each and stand in a row in front of the class, holding their digit cards so that the rest of the class can see. Replace one student's digit card with a decimal point card to create a mixed decimal. The rest of the class will then read the number the team creates.

Point out that the decimal point is read as "and." For example:

13.782 "Thirteen AND seven hundred eighty-two thousandths"

1.3782 "One AND three thousand seven hundred eighty-two ten-thousandths"

When the class correctly identifies the number, ask the decimal-point holder to move to a new position and have the class read the new number.

Continue in the same way until all teams have had a chance to create a mixed decimal.

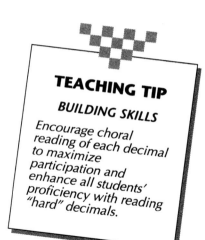

TEACHING TIP

BUILDING SKILLS

Encourage choral reading of each decimal to maximize participation and enhance all students' proficiency with reading "hard" decimals.

Wrapping Up

Write About Math: Using a grid paper transparency and an overhead projector, write a mixed decimal like 5.20. Write a number in each square and allow the decimal point its own square.

Have students write in their math journals the same decimal in numerals, in words, and as a fraction. Continue in the same way for other decimals: 3.75 and 4.625.

Lesson 7 — COMPARE AND ORDER DECIMALS

Materials
- digit and decimal point cards from lesson 6

Advance Preparation

This game is a follow-up to the activity in lesson 6. Plan to conduct it on the following day.

Organize two sets of digit cards. Two teams at a time will be forming decimals with the cards. The class will compare and order the decimals, as shown in the example below.

Which team has created the greater number? How can Team 2 rearrange its numbers to be greater?

48 Using Fractions, Decimals and Percent

Objectives
- to model, read, and write decimal numbers
- to compare and order decimal numbers

Getting Started
Assign two teams, each consisting of five students. Distribute a digit card to each of four students in each team. Give a decimal point card to the fifth student in each team.

Compare and Order Decimals
Have each team form a decimal number, holding up the cards for the class to see. Both teams should display their numbers at the same time.

Ask the rest of the class to read the two decimals and decide which team has created the greater decimal. Ask the students to explain how they know which one is greater. Then have them calculate the difference between the two decimal numbers.

Assign new teams and play additional rounds of the game.

Wrapping Up
After playing a few rounds of the game, ask students to describe their strategies for creating big numbers using these decimal cards.

Write About Math: Have students write responses in their math journals to the following prompts:
1. *What is the greatest number you can create with four different numerals and a decimal point? Explain how you know it is the greatest.*
2. *What is the second greatest number you can create with the same numerals? Explain your answer.*

TEACHING TIP

MEETING INDIVIDUAL NEEDS

Students who lack confidence in their decimal reading skills are likely to volunteer to hold the cards. Have student volunteers play the first round of the game. Then choose students at random for subsequent rounds. That way, everyone will get practice reading numbers.

Lesson 8: ESTIMATE AND ORDER DECIMALS

Materials
- digit and decimal point cards from lesson 6
- calculators
- overhead projector or chart paper

Advance Preparation

For this activity, students will try to form decimal numbers that are close to given target numbers.

Prepare a list of several target numbers that are two-digit whole numbers, such as 25, 36, and 94.

Objectives
- to compare and order decimals with reference to a benchmark
- to explore subtracting decimals using absolute value
- to assess students' understanding of decimals

Getting Started
Explain to students that they will work in teams to play a game called "Target Number." In this game, they try to form decimals as close as possible to a target number. Then they decide which group gets closer to the target number.

Form teams of five players. Give each team a set of digit cards.

Estimate and Order Decimals
Explain that you have a mystery target number and that each team will try to form a decimal that rounds to the target number. Have each team draw five digit cards at random.

Reveal the target number. Allow a few minutes for each team to form a decimal that is closest to the given number using all five digit cards and a decimal point. Write each team's solution on an overhead transparency or on chart paper. Then have each team decide which decimal is closest to the target number.

Have the team members use calculators to find out how much they would have to add or subtract to their number to reach the target number. Let the class decide (or confirm) which team's number is closest to the target number.

Play several rounds of the game.

TEACHING TIP

REACHING ALL LEARNERS

Use a number line to help visual learners see the location of the target number as it relates to the other decimals.

Round off decimals to help students estimate their positions on the number line.

Wrapping Up
As you discuss the results, have students order the decimals and target numbers from least to greatest. Then ask: "Which team's number is closest and which is farthest away from the target number? How do you know?" Demonstrate that a number that overshoots the target number may be closer than those that are less than the number.

Write About Math: Ask students to write about the games planned in this lesson and in lesson 6. They might indicate whether they liked each game and why, explain any strategies they used, and tell what they learned about decimals by playing the games.

What Really Happened

The "Target Numbers" game was great fun for all and helped bring together estimation, reading, writing, and number sense skills. It was gratifying to see how much students learned about decimals as they played the game.

Students used calculators to find the difference between the target number and the closest decimal numbers. Teams that formed decimals greater than the target number entered the target number first, subtracted the mixed decimal to find the difference, and noticed that their calculators gave negative numbers. We used this opportunity to introduce the concept of absolute value.

Sharing Ideas and Strategies

The homework assignment called for students to reflect on both games—"Follow the Bouncing Decimal Point" and "Target Numbers." Their responses showed how far students had come in their understanding of decimals. The assignment therefore provided a suitable assessment.

> I think that todays decimal game was a lot of fun. Its berry educational too. But I think the target numbers should not only be whole numbers but decimals also.
>
> Our stradegy was only for a couple numbers, mostly for 0 and 9. We thought they were good numbers to have because, when you wanted the number to be closer to the next you would put 9 after the decimal point. When you wanted the number to be closest to the last number you put 0 after the decimal point, we wanted to have those numbers for security.

Above, Julie described how to use zero and nine to get ahead in this game.

> **Follow the Bouncing Point**
>
> I liked the game because it was fun to try and form numbers. Our stratiegie was to always keep a zero out. Also to have a five because it's low but it rounds up.

Many students described strategies concerning which numbers were useful. At left, Maggie explained that a five rounds up.

Below, Lauren backed up her strategy with a detailed explanation of how the game works.

> Our table had a couple of strategies on choosing decimal cards:
>
> 1) Always have a nine so that if you don't have one # you need out of a two digit #, you could round easily. (it's kind of hard to explain)
>
> 2) Usually have a zero in case you have the whole # part exact. Then you could just put a .0........ chances are, your # wouldn't round anywhere.
>
> 3) Usually have a 5
>
> Say the number was 50, and you had the #'s
>
> 4, 9, 5, 1, 2
>
> you could put 49.512
> the 5 means ½, so your # would round up to 50!

Follow the decimal ball.

Yes, I liked the follow the decimal ball game! I think that It's fun, but challenging. You really should use it in the future — it's very creative, and unique! My team didn't really have a strategy, but we figured out your pattern, going big number, small number.

Sonya illustrated her answer. She demonstrated that she had learned about absolute value playing the decimals games.

DECIMALS, FRACTIONS, AND MONEY

SECTION 4

LESSON 9: MAKE A TIME LINE LITERATURE CONNECTION: *THE STORY OF MONEY* BY BETSY MAESTRO	56
LESSON 10: FIND PERCENTS	62
LESSON 11: PICTURE DECIMALS	64
LESSON 12: THE ANTS' PICNIC	66
LESSON 13: GET OFF THE FIELD!	70
EXTENSIONS AND HOMEWORK	72

Lesson 9: Make a Time Line

Materials

- ***The Story of Money*** by Betsy Maestro
- **Data Sheet from *The Story of Money*,** S-7
- **Plan Your Time Line,** S-8
- social studies books or other reference books with time lines of the evolution of human culture
- rulers
- 18" x 24" paper (one sheet for each pair of students)
- colored markers (optional)
- overhead projector

Advance Preparation

Go through social studies or other reference books and choose several time lines for the class discussion. Note the scales of these time lines.

Make copies of **Data Sheet from *The Story of Money*,** S-7 and **Plan Your Time Line,** S-8, for each student.

Plan Your Time Line

EXAMINE A SAMPLE TIME LINE

1. What data does the sample time line show?

2. What period of time does the sample time line cover?

3. What intervals does the sample use?

4. What scale does the sample use?

CHECK YOUR DATA FROM *THE STORY OF MONEY*

1. What data will your time line show? Give your time line a title.

2. What period of time does your time line cover?

   About how many years are between the period of early man and the Sumerians?

   About how many years are between the Sumerians and the Lydians?

   About how many years are between the Lydian culture and Marco Polo's visit to China?

3. What intervals will you mark? Think about the size of your paper. How will you fit in the data?

4. What scale will you use to fit your data onto the paper? How did you decide?

Data Sheet from *The Story of Money*

Read ***The Story of Money*.** Find information in the book that will help you make a time line. Write it in the boxes below.

Who?	Dates	Kind of economy	What did they use for money?
Early peoples (before Catal Huyuk)	2,500,000 B.C.	hunters/gatherers	They didn't need any.
People of Catal Huyuk			
Sumerian traders			
Lydian traders			
Chinese empire at the time of Marco Polo			
Spanish Empire			
Colonial America			
The early United States			
Money today			

Using Fractions, Decimals and Percent

Objectives

- to collect data from a storybook
- to make a time line from chronological data
- to use ideas of scale to make a time line

Getting Started

Explain that in this unit, students will be learning about decimals, fractions, and percent. Ask questions like, "Where in your everyday life do you use decimals? When do you need to know about percent?" Elicit that people use decimals when they use money and that percent is frequently related to consumer experiences like shopping.

Now ask, "What do you use for money?" Elicit that we have paper money and coins (usually made of copper and nickel). Elicit that people use other forms of money such as credit cards and checks.

Make a Time Line

Distribute recording sheets (S-7) to each student. Explain to students that these worksheets will be helpful as a tool to record information from their reading and that they will eventually make a time line with this information. Display a copy on the overhead. Begin by reading aloud the first few pages of **The Story of Money**. After you read pages 3–7, ask students questions that will help fill in the worksheet. For example,

> "What kinds of civilizations are described on pages 3 to 7? When might these people have lived? What information on page 6 could you use in a time line?"

> "Where could you get information about when these people lived that would give you a way to start a time line?"

Wrapping Up

Display the sample time lines that show how other illustrators have met the challenge of representing time. Compare scales chosen for different time lines. Then group the students in pairs. Make sure each pair has a sample time line to study closely. Assign **Plan Your Time Line,** S-8, to help students plan and create their time lines showing data from **The Story of Money.**

LITERATURE CONNECTION

The Story of Money by Betsy Maestro

Who?	Dates	Kind of economy	What did they use for money?
Early peoples (before Catal Huyuk)	2,500,000 B.C.	hunters/gatherers	they didn't need any
People of Catal Huyuk	10,000 B.C.	farmers/gatherers trade	furs food salt obsidian
Sumerian traders	3,000 B.C.	traders	barley/silver
Lydian traders			
Chinese empire at the time of Marco Polo			
Spanish Empire			
Colonial America			
The early United States			
Money today			

Help students organize the information they need to complete their time lines.

What Really Happened

We began by working together as a whole group to evaluate some examples of time lines from our social studies books. Students easily saw that the interval on a time line was like a scale; one example showed intervals of 50 years. Another showed 200-year intervals. Students also knew how to calculate the period of years covered in sample time lines. (All of the examples we examined were horizontal time lines.)

Students' responses indicated that they were ready to make their own time lines.

Some students needed help starting to fill in worksheet S-7. They needed to be reminded to keep math in mind. "As you read, make a list that includes information you will need to make a time line."

After students recorded data from the book, some needed help planning a scale for their time lines. They knew they were going to fit the entire time line on one piece of construction paper.

When we asked students "What scale will you use for your time line?", several groups pointed out that it was hard to figure a scale for all the dates covered because the time line had to cover 2,502,000 years!

"We tried to use two million as an interval. That gets rid of two million years but then there is no way to show all the detail later on," Louise and Chrissy pointed out.

We called all groups to attention and asked whether anyone else had found a solution to this problem.

"It won't work! We can't find a measure that will fit!"

"You'd have to have a bigger piece of paper."

"It would go on for miles!"

After a brief discussion we agreed to exclude the most remote date from our time lines. Several students pointed out that what people used for money didn't really change much over that time.

Building a time line from a set of data where the time intervals are irregular was a challenge for many students. They knew that they needed to find a scale, but many students did not relate the scale to the number of years their data covered.

TEACHING TIP

USING CRITICAL THINKING: OBSERVATION SKILLS

Suggest that students look for examples of time lines in their social studies textbook. Have students make a list of the characteristics of a time line.

As an alternative, make copies of "Civilizations Fact Sheet" available for students to use as they read the book.

Jeremy, Ryo, and Andre decided they needed ten segments in their time line because there were ten sets of data on the recording sheet! They measured the width of the paper, found that there was enough length to make 2-inch segments and measured off enough 2-inch segments to fill the page. Then they entered the data from their recording sheets without regard for the period of time that separated the data.

When we discussed the discrepancy, they acknowledged their time line was not to scale, but they did not want to start again.

Courtney had started a time line with 1,000-year intervals. As we returned to see how she was progressing in placing her data, we noticed that she had made some drastic changes. We asked why she had changed her scale.

"Well, if I used this 1,000-year scale, most of my time line would be blank. Everything would show up on one side of the paper."

"So what interval will you use?"

"I'm just going to make the sections even so that there is stuff everywhere on my paper."

We pointed out that this strategy would not result in a time line. "If you use a scale, you'll see one of the interesting things about money. For thousands of years people didn't need money. One of the things a time line can show is how human inventions cluster in a short period of time."

"OK," Courtney said. "I get it." She revised her time line using her original scale.

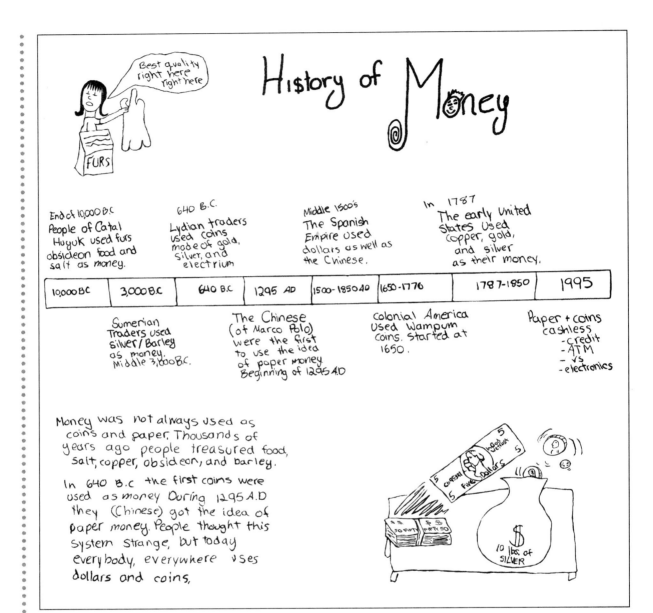

Lisa's time line, shown above, had all items in proper sequence. She shared much from her research and did wonderful illustrations. However, her time line is not to scale. In a discussion, she realized she had not included her ideas of scale. After thinking it over, she decided not to redo her time line.

Julie's group created a time line that was to scale. Then they discovered they wanted to devote more space to the most recent 2,000 years. When we pointed out this might confuse someone using the time line, they decided to create a "magnified square" to give enough space from A.D. 200 to 2000. Their time line is on the facing page.

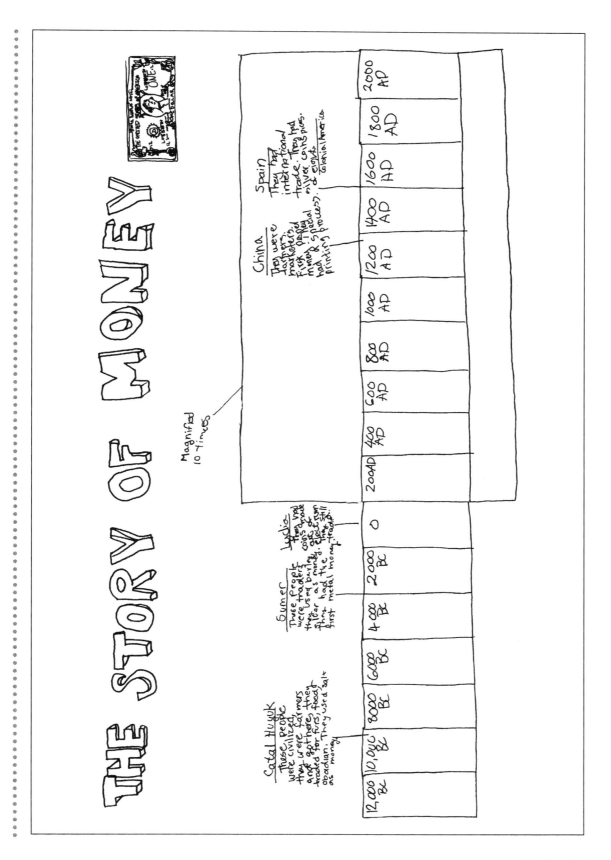

Lesson 10 — FIND PERCENTS

Materials

- **Picture Parts of a Dollar**, S-9
- **Find Percents,** S-10
- overhead transparency
- overhead projector

Advance Preparation

Make a transparency of **Picture Parts of a Dollar**, S-9. Make a copy of **Finding Percents**, S-10, for each student.

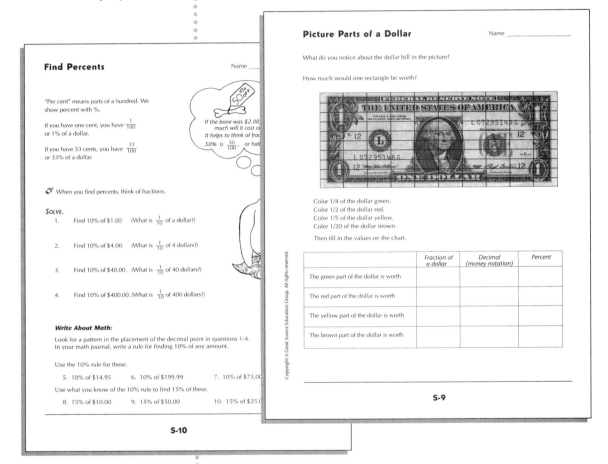

62 Using Fractions, Decimals and Percent

Objectives
- to understand percent concepts
- to represent percents as fractions and decimals
- to find easy percents of quantities

Getting Started
Tell students that in this lesson they will learn how percents, fractions, and decimals are related. Ask, "What do you know about percent? Where do we use percent?" Elicit that percent means "parts per hundred."

Find Percents
Work with the whole class. Display the transparency of **Picture Parts of a Dollar,** S-9. Discuss students' observations. Complete the chart. Then have students work with a partner to complete **Find Percents,** S-10.

Wrapping Up
Discuss results as a class.

Extension/Homework
Have students find sale brochures or catalogs and calculate the sale price for three items they might buy. Then have them determine how much money they would save.

TEACHING TIP

MAKING CONNECTIONS

Students generally have good intuition about percent from their own experiences. Ask, "If you wanted to buy a jacket for $50, and it was marked 50% off, how much would it cost?" ($25) Suppose it was marked 10% off? ($45), 25% off? ($37.50)

Lesson 11: PICTURE DECIMALS

Materials

- **Picture Decimals with Centimeter Squares,** S-11
- **Parts of Decimals,** S-12
- **More Parts of Decimals,** S-13
- **Challenge: Find the Whole from the Part,** S-14
- overhead projector
- overhead transparency
- digit and decimal point cards from lesson 6
- rulers
- colored pencils (or markers)
- chart paper marked into cm or inch grid

Advance Preparation

Make a transparency of **Picture Decimals with Centimeter Squares,** S-11.

Make copies of **Parts of Decimals,** S-12; **More parts of Decimals,** S-13; and **Challenge: Find the Whole from the Part,** S-14.

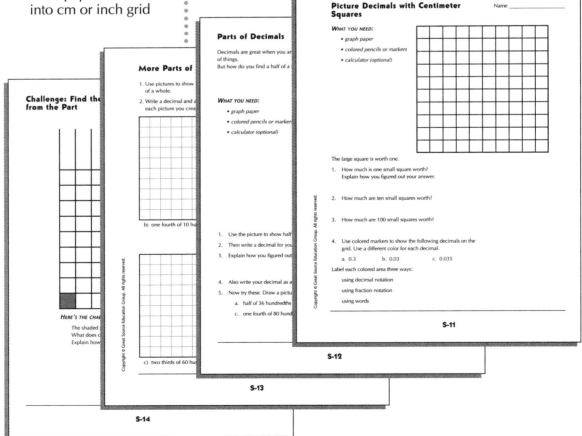

Objectives

- to represent decimal amounts using a hundredth square chart
- to recognize the relationship between decimals and fractions

Getting Started

Play a few rounds of "Follow the Bouncing Decimal Point" (pages 46–47). Then tell students that today they will practice picturing decimals and writing parts of a whole as decimals, as fractions, in words, and in exponential notation.

Display the transparency of **Picture Decimals with Centimeter Squares,** S-11. Ask students to take a few minutes to jot down everything they notice about the illustration in their math journal. Then have them share their ideas. If students have difficulty coming up with statements, offer the following prompts:

"Think about what you know about decimals. What decimal ideas can you show on a grid like this?"

"Think about what you know about fractions. What ideas about fractions can you show on a grid like this?"

Eventually, students should recognize that each small square represents 1/100 of the whole large square.

Picture Decimals

Distribute copies of S-11 through S-14 to the class. Provide rulers and colored pencils or markers to groups of students to share. Then have students work independently or with a partner to complete these pages.

Circulate throughout the classroom and observe students as they work. Coach as needed.

Wrapping Up

Gather the class for discussion. Call on volunteers to share their solutions and strategies.

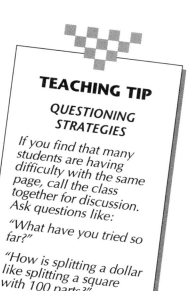

TEACHING TIP

QUESTIONING STRATEGIES

If you find that many students are having difficulty with the same page, call the class together for discussion. Ask questions like:

"What have you tried so far?"

"How is splitting a dollar like splitting a square with 100 parts?"

Lesson 12 — THE ANTS' PICNIC

Materials

- *One Hundred Hungry Ants* by Elinor Pinczes, optional (See Bibliography on page 133.)
- **The Ants' Picnic,** S-15
- **Tinier and Tinier,** S-16
- centimeter graph paper
- metric rulers
- colored pencils or markers
- calculators (optional)

Advance Preparation

Make a copy of **The Ants' Picnic**, S-15, and **Tinier and Tinier**, S-16, for each student.

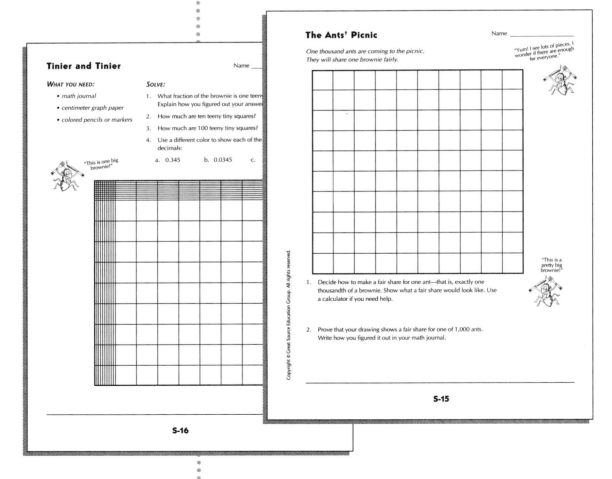

66   Using Fractions, Decimals and Percent

Objectives
- to explore pictorial representations for decimals
- to relate decimal ideas and ideas about fractions

Getting Started

LITERATURE OPTION: Before you read aloud *One Hundred Hungry Ants*, explain to the class that this is a story for younger students but one with interesting illustrations. Tell them they will be rating it as a book for younger readers.

Read the story and then go back and study some of the illustrations. For each page, ask students to identify a fraction, a decimal, and a percent for each division of the ants. Explain that students will try to figure out what a fair share of a brownie looks like for 1,000 ants.

The Ants' Picnic

Distribute copies of **The Ants' Picnic,** S-15, and **Tinier and Tinier,** S-16. Allow time for students to read the instructions. Field questions. Then have students work individually or in pairs to solve the problems.

Circulate throughout the classroom. Observe and coach students as they work. Encourage students to describe their solution strategies clearly and in detail so that someone else might be able to replicate their method.

Wrapping Up

Invite students to share their solutions and their problem-solving strategies. Have students show one portion of the brownie as a picture, as a fraction, as a decimal, and in exponential notation.

Write About Math: Have students write a critique of *One Hundred Hungry Ants* as a storybook for younger readers and as a picture book that illustrates ideas of fractions and decimals.

TEACHING TIP

QUESTIONING STRATEGIES

If students are having difficulty, ask questions like:

"What have you tried so far?"

"How would using metric measurements help you?"

"What would 1/10 of the brownie look like? How could you use your ruler to show fair shares?"

"What would 1/100 of the brownie look like?"

"What could you do to make thousandths out of hundredths?"

TEACHING TIP

SHARING IDEAS

If students have difficulty with the activity, gather the class together for discussion. Ask students to share their progress so far; for example, how they got started and where they ran into difficulty.

What Really Happened

This activity did not seem very successful when we used it the first time. We include it here, however, because it did provide an unexpected, informal assessment of connections students were and were not making between place value concepts and their applications. Very few students made the connection!

Students tried different methods of solving the problem. Making 100 shares was fairly obvious to most students. However, getting from 100 to 1,000 shares was a challenge. Students realized that they had to divide the hundredths again. However, most students cut a sample square into 100 smaller pieces and made ten-thousandths rather than thousandths. How to combine ten-thousandths into pieces that measure one-thousandth of the brownie was surprisingly difficult.

One student computed the area of the brownie and then divided by 1,000. Although this strategy was excellent mathematically, he couldn't envision what one piece would look like.

Other students began by cutting the brownie into halves, fourths, eighths, sixteenths, and so on. By using a calculator, these students discovered that this strategy would eventually result in 1028 portions—28 pieces more than they needed for the 1,000 ants.

We called for class discussion to get students "unstuck." Several students thought that the size of the brownie (15 cm by 15 cm) was not very helpful. They suggested that making it 10 cm by 10 cm would make the problem easier. Others disagreed, saying that they still didn't see why a teeny tiny square was not the right answer. We challenged students to evaluate why their answer was not right—to give the problem one more try.

Jane, right, calculated a correct numerical answer but did not understand how to show that result as an area of a brownie.

> Sides: 15 cm. each.
> Area: 225 square cm.
>
> First I measured the sides which are each 15 cm. Then I figured out the area which is 225 cm. I divided that by a thousand to find out the area of one thousanth.

Using Fractions, Decimals and Percent

Sharing Ideas and Strategies

Maggie, right, could write about the numbers. However, like Jane, she could not show what that portion would look like.

> The Ants Picnic
> On this work sheet I was asked a question, the question is How did you figure this out? What I did is this...
>
> × 1000 - one thousand ants
> 1 - one ant
> ———
> 1000
>
> after doing that it told me that each ant needed one thousandth of the brownie. So the size would be about this big →
> □

Louise, left, took a practical approach. However, when asked to apply her strategy to show what a piece would look like, she ran into division difficulties.

> First I needed to find out what numbers equal 1,000. I know that 100 multiplied by 10 = 1,000 but I would hate to draw 1,000 lines so I found another problem that would equal 1,000 which is 50 × 20 so I would draw 20 lines one way and 50 lines the other way and get 1/1000 of a piece of that brownie.

> The square or brownie is 15 cm by 15 cm. To figure out how small each thousenth of that square is you devide 15 cm by 1,000. The answer is 0.01. That meens that each square will be 0.015 cm by 0.015 cm.

*Nate tried applying ideas of linear measurement. However, his method results in 100 × 100 pieces or **ten**-thousandths.*

Lesson 13: GET OFF THE FIELD!

Materials

- cardstock copies of **Get Off the Field!**, page 118
- **How to Play Get Off the Field!**, S-17
- **Recording Sheet for Get Off the Field!**, S-18
- *If You Made a Million* by David M. Schwartz, optional (See Bibliography on page 133.)
- scissors
- calculators (optional)

Advance Preparation

Copy page 118 on heavyweight cardstock, if possible. This will make the game pieces more durable and easier to handle. You will need one copy for each group of two to four students.

Make one copy of **How to Play Get Off the Field!**, S-17, for each group. Make a copy of **Recording Sheet for Get Off the Field!**, S-18, for each student.

Decide whether to allow students to use calculators as they work.

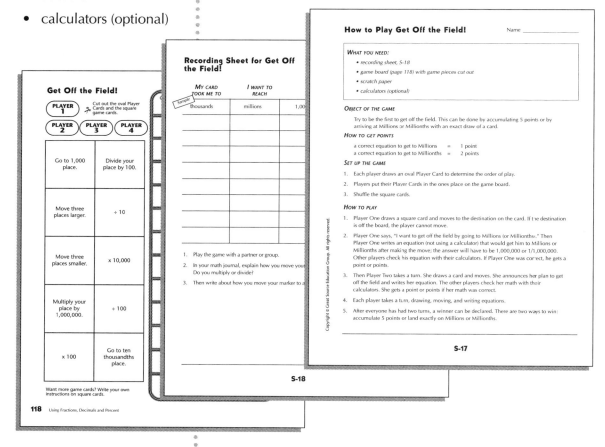

70 Using Fractions, Decimals and Percent

Objectives

- to recognize place value from billions to billionths
- to write multiplication and division equations using whole numbers and decimals
- to relate positive and negative exponential numbers to their place value

Getting Started

If you wish, review large numbers by reading *If You Made a Million* to your class. Write *1,000,000* on the board. Ask students what it would be called if you add a zero to this number (10 million). Also review 100 million and one billion (which the British call one thousand million). Write one millionth on the board ($\frac{1}{1,000,000}$) and ask students how to write one billionth.

Now introduce the game. Have students form groups of two to four players. Give each group a cardstock copy of page 118.

Get Off the Field!

Read the game instructions, provided on S-17, as a class. Answer any questions the students may have. Make sure students understand which items are the player markers, game cards, and playing field. Provide scissors and let one player in each group cut apart the game cards and player markers, keeping the rest of the page intact.

As students play the game, have them record their moves, equations, and points on S-18.

Circulate throughout the classroom and observe students as they play.

Wrapping Up

Discuss strategies that students discovered to decide how to be the first to get off the field.

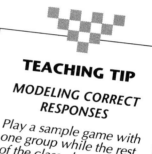

TEACHING TIP

MODELING CORRECT RESPONSES

Play a sample game with one group while the rest of the class observes and offers help. This will give reluctant players a chance to see how to make moves during the game.

EXTENSIONS AND HOMEWORK

1. Have students make a time line of the twentieth century that will fit on a piece of graph paper. (Allow ten decades.) Tell them to mark the end of each decade on the time line: 1910, 1920, 1930, etc. They can write in the birth dates of family members and other family milestones on the time line.

2. Students can create circle graphs about the composition of U.S. coins using the data in the teaching tip on this page. They can create a circle for pennies, one for nickels, and one each for dimes, quarters, and dollar coins.

3. Have students research the price of three restaurant meals, then calculate the tip: (For average service, add 15 percent to the total: For excellent service, add 20 percent to the total.)

4. Ask students to research the sales tax that people pay in their community. They can make a list of five items that they would like to buy. Have them use a calculator to compute the sales tax for each item, and then write the total they would pay.

5. Assign students to cut out newspaper stories that use numbers larger than one million. Have them practice reading them aloud. Then they can report on how to make sense of large numbers.

One student we know analyzes the U.S. budget this way. He divides the big budget number (for example: $1 billion) by the number of people in the United States (about 250 million). Our example yields 4 dollars per person, which is an easier number to understand.

TEACHING TIP

BACKGROUND INFORMATION

Nickels are made of 75% copper and 25% nickel.

Pennies are made of bronze (95% copper and 5% zinc).

Dimes, quarters, and dollars are made of about 80% copper and 20% nickel.

The government stopped using gold in coins in 1934. Dimes and quarters lost their silver content in 1965.

CAR BUYER'S PROJECT

PROJECT OVERVIEW   74

LESSON 14: PHASE I   76

    PLAN TO BUY A CAR

    LEARN TO READ ADS

    MAKE A PAYMENT PLAN

LESSON 15: PHASE II   80

    DEVELOP A MONTHLY BUDGET

LESSON 16: GRAPH YOUR BUDGET   84

LESSON 17: PHASE III   86

    COMPUTE THE RESALE VALUE OF YOUR CAR

    MAKE AN AD TO SELL YOUR CAR

LESSON 18: STUDENT SELF-EVALUATION   90

Project Overview

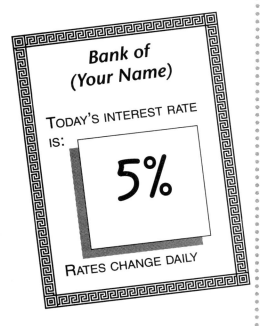

Projects are a great teaching tool. When students are engaged in projects they get a chance to see how the math applies to real world situations. The project format gives you an opportunity to assess how well your students solve problems and apply their understanding of fractions, decimals and percent. This is a time to set aside your expectations about pen-and-pencil arithmetic. Make calculators available, and watch your students blossom as real-world problem solvers.

This is a good time to be a bit of a ham. We've even suggested a script idea that you might want to use to set the tone for this project in your classroom. (See **Presentation Scenario**, page 78.)

To prepare for the role-playing, plan for the following:

- a classroom set of calculators

- a place to post the daily interest rate (see **Advance Preparation,** page 76). We created a small sign for students to check each day. We told students that the daily interest rate would change and so they would have to check it each day and make adjustments as they figured the loan payments on their chosen cars.

- a simple spreadsheet on a classroom computer to verify students' calculations on their Car Buyer's Loan Worksheets. You may want to designate a daily Loan Officer in charge of using the spreadsheet to check the worksheets that have been submitted that day. If the worksheet checks out, stamp it "approved." Worksheets that do not check out should be stamped "oops!" and returned to students to recalculate. Be sure that your spreadsheet is updated each day to reflect the new daily interest rate.

- the automobile section from recent classified ad sections of the paper. You may want to ask students to bring in classified ad sections of the paper ahead of time so that each student has a section to scan. If the automobile section of your paper is large, one paper may suffice for several students.

CAR BUYER'S PROJECT • PHASE I

Students will use data from classified advertisements to identify three used cars, one in each price category: less than $10,000, between $10,000 and $20,000, and more than $20,000.

Then students will fill out a Car Buyer's Loan Worksheet for each car they have chosen. They will calculate the amount of money they need to borrow from the bank and the monthly payment that would be due on each car.

CAR BUYER'S PROJECT • PHASE II

Students will choose a career at random from the "Career Bank." Based on the indicated annual income, they will develop a personal monthly budget that includes monthly payments on the car appropriate for their income level.

Integrating Language Arts: Students write an imaginative Lifestyle Essay in which they describe their jobs, their daily routines, and their financial decisions.

Graphing Activity: Students create bar graphs and circle graphs to represent their budgets.

Students can create a Project Portfolio with a creative cover. In it, they present their worksheets, their monthly budgets, their Lifestyle Essay, and their graphs.

CAR BUYER'S PROJECT • PHASE III

Imagining that they have owned their car for three years, students will calculate the resale value of their car and develop a classified ad to resell their car at a fair market value.

They add these items to their portfolios.

PROJECT SELF-EVALUATION

Students review elements of the project and evaluate their performance and their learning.

MENTAL MATH WARM-UPS

Plan to use one or more Mental Math Warm-Ups with upcoming lessons to keep math skills sharp on project days. The Mental Math Warm-Ups on pages 125-132 in this book are closely linked to the Car Buyer's Project.

Make transparencies of the Mental Math Warm-Up pages and display them on the overhead. Ask students what they notice or what they think they need to figure out.

Or, make copies of the Mental Math Warm-Ups and assign them as homework or classwork.

Lesson 14 — CAR BUYER'S PROJECT
PHASE I

Materials

- **Sample Car Ads,** page 119
- **Car Buyer's Project • Phase I,** S-19
- **Car Buyer's Loan Worksheet,** S-20
- **Mental Math Warm-Up/Find Percents • 1,** page 125
- classified ads from the local paper
- overhead projector
- overhead transparency
- overhead marker
- scissors
- tape or glue
- calculators
- chart paper
- marker
- Blue Book

Advance Preparation

Collect classified advertising sections from your local newspaper. Gather enough so that each student will have a page of car ads to work with.

Make transparencies of **Sample Car Ads** (page 119) and **Car Buyer's Loan Worksheet,** S-20, to demonstrate the activity. Prepare a transparency of **Mental Math Warm-Up**, page 125.

Make a copy of **Car Buyers Project • Phase 1**, S-19, for each student. Make four copies per student of **Car Buyer's Loan Worksheet,** S-20.

Prepare a Daily Interest Rate chart with today's interest rate (sample: 5%). You will vary rates over several class periods, so a rising interest rate may motivate students to complete Phase I of the project.

If you have access to a computer, set up a simple spreadsheet to facilitate checking students' calculations on their **Car Buyer's Loan Worksheets.**

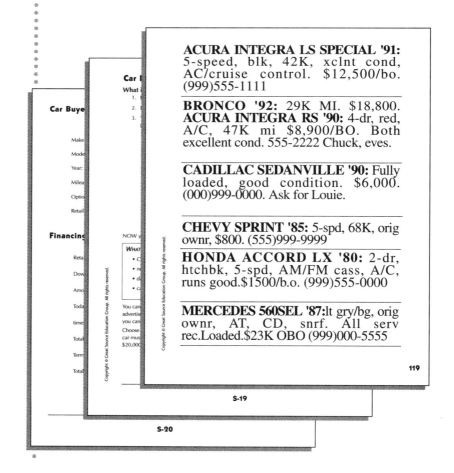

76 Using Fractions, Decimals, and Percent

Objectives

- to understand information in newspaper ads
- to use information from an advertisement
- to compare and order large numbers
- to apply decimal concepts in a real-world setting

Getting Started

Tell students that over the next two weeks they will have class time to complete the Car Buyer's Project. Explain that this is a project in three phases. In Phase I, they will be looking through advertisements for cars to buy. In Phase II, they will draw a career out of a hat and develop a personal budget, including car payments.

Display a transparency of **Mental Math Warm-Up**, page 125, and complete it with the students.

Car Buyer's Project • Phase I

Introduce the activity. Use the Presentation Scenario and step-by-step guidelines on page 78. Be sure to make time to discuss the language of classified advertisements. Also make time to fill out **Car Buyer's Loan Worksheet,** S-20, together with your students. Coach as needed for finding percents using a calculator, rounding money amounts to the nearest penny, and appropriate operations for determining the amount to finance and the total monthly payment.

Then have students work independently to choose ads from the newspaper, tape their ad to a **Car Buyer's Loan Worksheet,** and fill out the data for approval by the bank. Circulate around the classroom, coaching as needed.

Wrapping Up

Have students hand in their work. Act as the loan officer, approving worksheets if they are done correctly.

Extension/Homework

Have students research the value of their chosen used cars using the **Blue Book** (available in public libraries and at car dealerships). Have them compare the asking price in their ads with the range of asking prices in the **Blue Book**.

Mental Math Answer Key		
Find 10 Percent:		
1. 10	2. 3	3. 4.5
4. 22.7	5. 55.5	6. 200
7. .052	8. .03	9. .007
Find 15 Percent:		
1. 15	2. 150	3. 225
4. 3.75	5. 7.35	6. 49.95

Presentation Scenario

Robin introduced the activity to her sixth-grade students with the following real-life scenario.

> A few years ago, I decided that I really needed a new car, so I asked my father to buy me one. And he said, "No!" So I asked my Aunt Charmaine to buy me one and she said, "No!" I asked a few more people I knew well and everyone said, "No!" Then my dad said, "You should ask the bank."
>
> So I went to the bank and they said, "Let's talk about it. We think that because you are a teacher with a steady job, you are a good risk. So we will lend you the money. You have to put up 10% of the price of the car, and we will lend you the rest of the money. All you have to do is agree to pay the interest rate-of-the-day that we make you the loan."
>
> I figured out pretty quickly that I couldn't afford a new car. Then I looked in the newspaper for used cars. I had to decide what to buy.

Buying a Car Step-by-Step

Distribute a copy of **Car Buyer's Project • Phase I** (S-19) to each student. Then explain that students will be looking for car ads of their own, using classified advertisements from the newspaper. They need to find at least three different cars that they might buy— at least one that costs under $10,000, at least one that costs between $10,000 and $20,000, and at least one that costs more than $20,000. This is important because they will have to choose the car they can afford in Phase II from their approved Payment Plans, completed in Phase I. They may prepare Payment Plans for as many cars as they like, as long as at least one car falls into each price category.

Then display a transparency of **Sample Car Ads,** page 119. Ask students what information they can get from the ad. Make a list of advertising abbreviations and what they mean. Invite students to add to the list as they look for their own ads.

Distribute a **Car Buyer's Loan Worksheet,** S-20, to each student. Explain that for each car students choose, they will need to fill out a **Car Buyer's Loan Worksheet.** Display a copy of S-20 on the overhead and explain each line item. Then work together with students to complete a worksheet, using the information from the **Sample Car Ads.**

Make available the newspaper advertising sections along with a stack of ready-to-fill **Car Buyer's Loan Worksheets.** Students will complete one worksheet for each car they research. Remind students that the interest rate at the bank will change each day.

What Really Happened

Students had little difficulty figuring out the year of the advertised cars. They enjoyed deciphering the meaning of abbreviations like "snrf" (sunroof) and "bo" (best offer). When we told them that newspapers charge by the line for classified ads, students began to understand the value of being brief. Students who knew about cars had a lot to contribute to the conversation.

We developed a chart of car buyer's abbreviations. We encouraged students to add to the list daily, giving abbreviations and translations.

Over the next three class periods, students had about 45 minutes a day to develop **Car Buyer's Loan Worksheets.** This provided us ample opportunity to circulate and coach students in needed skills as they figured out what each line item meant. Many students wanted to round the outcomes to the nearest dollar. We explained that because the bank wanted to know **to the penny** what a fair monthly payment would be, students should round only to the nearest cent.

A few students needed coaching as they tried to figure out how the line items on the loan worksheets were related. Students had to be reminded that since they were taking out a four-year loan, their monthly payment would be 1/48 of the total financed amount. (In our lesson with a three-year loan, we are calculating 1/36 of the financed amount.) In the seven years we have taught this unit, students have never commented on our class bank's generosity. To keep interest rate computations simple, the class bank charges 8% for three years, not 8% each year as would happen in the real world.

We set up a simple spreadsheet on our single classroom computer to check students' calculations. Giving students plenty of class time to prepare loan worksheets also gave us time to check their computations and give almost immediate feedback. Some students had to recalculate their worksheets two or three times before they found a correct payment for their chosen car. Making corrections to their worksheets provided excellent practice and helped students gain insights into the underlying math concepts.

Changing the interest rates daily helped students stay on task. If worksheets were turned in a day late, students had to recalculate their figures based on the new daily interest rate.

Car Buyer's Abbreviations

4-dr	four door
xlnt	excellent
4wd	four wheel drive
snrf	sunroof
str	stereo
K	thousand (mileage)
AT	automatic transmission
ac	air conditioning
dlr	dealer
sac	sacrifice
rblt eng	rebuilt engine
cc	cruise control
lthr	leather
mi	miles
lks	looks
rns	runs
nu	new
trs	tires
brks	brakes
gd cond	good condition
cltch	clutch
blk	black
PB	power brakes
ABS	anti-lock braking system

Lesson 15: Car Buyer's Project
Phase II

Materials

- **Mental Math Warm-Up/Find Percents • 2**, page 126
- **Monthly Budget Practice Sheet**, S-21
- **My Monthly Budget**, S-22
- **The Video Store Clerk's Budget**, page 120
- overhead transparency
- overhead projector
- **Career Descriptions**, pages 121–124
- shoebox or coffee tin
- calculators

For **Extension/Homework:**

- folders for each student
- **Car Buyer's Project • Phase II • Organize Your Work**, S-23

Advance Preparation

Prepare a transparency of **The Video Store Clerk's Budget**, page 120, to use as you present Phase II.

Prepare a transparency of **Mental Math Warm-Up**, page 126.

Make enough copies of each **Career Descriptions** (pages 121–124) to provide a variety of choices for your class. Cut the pages into thirds and place the career descriptions in your shoebox or coffee tin for the career drawing.

Make copies of **Monthly Budget Practice Sheet**, S-21; **My Monthly Budget**, S-22; and **Car Buyer's Project•Phase II •Organize Your Work**, S-23 for each student.

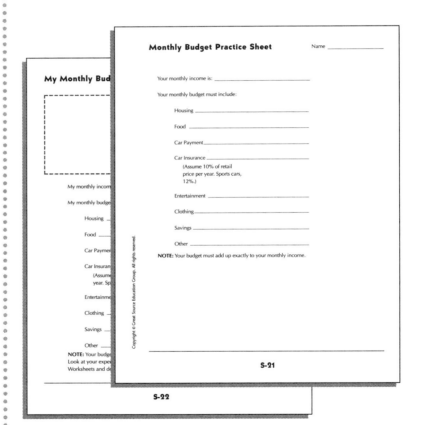

80 Using Fractions, Decimals, and Percent

Objectives

- to balance a budget
- to use money concepts
- to use percent concepts in a real-world setting

Getting Started

Explain to students that as soon as they complete Phase I, they will be drawing a career out of the box. Once they know what their career is, they will choose a car to buy from their approved loan applications developed in Phase I and develop a personal budget that includes a monthly car payment.

Display a transparency of **The Video Store Clerk's Budget,** page 120. Have students take notes on **Monthly Budget Practice Sheets,** S-21, as you work through this example with the class. (See the guidelines for presenting Phase II on page 82.)

Car Buyer's Project • Phase II

Display a transparency of **Mental Math Warm-Up**, page 126. Work through the page with the students. Then have students work independently to complete their loan applications. Have students, in turn, choose a career out of the box. Then they work out their monthly budgets and use **My Monthly Budget,** S-22, to record their final budgets.

Circulate and observe. Coach individuals or small groups as needed.

Wrapping Up

About five minutes before the end of math class, give students time to clean up their project and put it in a safe place for continuing work.

Extensions/Homework

After students have completed their budgets, distribute copies of **Car Buyer's Project • Phase II • Organize Your Work,** S-23.

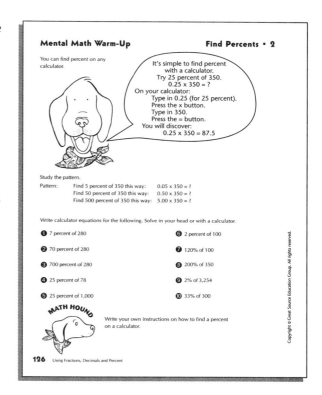

Mental Math Answer Key
1. 0.07 x 280 = 19.6
2. 0.70 x 280 = 196
3. 7.00 x 280 = 1960
4. 0.25 x 78 = 19.5
5. 0.25 x 1,000 = 250
6. 0.02 x 100 = 2
7. 1.20 x 100 = 120
8. 2.00 x 350 = 700
9. 0.02 x 3,254 = 65.08
10. 0.33 x 300 = 99

Presenting Phase II

Present this part of the project in a whole class setting as students complete approved **Car Buyer's Loan Worksheets.** Giving students a look at Phase II will motivate them to complete Phase I more efficiently.

Display the careers box. Explain that, as students complete approved **Car Buyer's Loan Worksheets,** they will be drawing a career at random. They might be brain surgeons earning lots of money or teachers earning less. They might be rock stars or secretaries. Their futures are in the box. Using the data from their career sheets, they will decide which car they can afford and develop a monthly budget that includes car payments.

Display a transparency of **The Video Store Clerk's Budget,** page 120. Have students tell you what they notice about the data sheet. Ask questions like,

"About what fraction of my total budget do I need for housing? How do you know?"

"About what fraction of my total budget do I need for food? How do you know?"

"Which car would you buy if you had this income? Why?"

"What fraction of my total budget would that car take up?"

With the class, work through each line item of the worksheet using the video clerk's income. Have students follow along with **Monthly Budget Practice Sheet,** S-21, making notes of equations they will need to use to calculate each line item. If possible, use a calculator for the overhead to demonstrate each calculation.

This is a good time to introduce how to use the percent key on the calculator.

What Really Happened

Several students who had had little experience working with calculators and were new to operating with percents were dividing the retail price by 10 or 12 to calculate their car insurance rather than multiplying the retail price by 0.10 or 0.12.

Mary had bought a car that cost $9,000. To find her insurance payment, she first tried multiplying $9,000 by 12 "since 'of' means 'times'." Her operations sense was good. But when the result of her multiplication didn't make sense, she decided she needed to divide by 12 instead. $9,000 ÷ 12 gave $600, which seemed to be a reasonable insurance rate. I worked with Mary and several other students who were making the same error.

"You were right the first time, when you knew that you should multiply," I told Mary. "Let's figure out what the correct multiplier is. I'm going to ask you some questions about finding percents of things first. Then we'll figure out what numbers to put in the calculator. Do you remember how to figure 10 percent of a price?"

"Sure! You just move the decimal point."

"So what would 10 percent of your retail price be?"

Mary thought for a minute. "It would be $900. That seems like an awful lot for insurance."

"That does sound expensive, but your math is right. 10 percent of $9,000 is $900. Now how much more do you have to pay for insurance?"

"I don't know. Two percent?"

"Why two percent?"

Mary shrugged, unwilling to go on.

"You had something in mind when you said two percent. I see a pattern that tells me you were thinking when you found that number." I wanted Mary to explain her reasoning.

"Well, I figured maybe if I already found 10 percent I could start with that and have to find 2 percent more."

"You are absolutely right! That's how it works. So what would you do next?"

Mary used her calculator's percent key to find that 2 percent of 9,000 = $180. She then added $900 and $180 to find her insurance rate of $1,080.

We noticed that many students were using the percent key to find their car insurance. We reminded the class to check that their car insurance should be at least 10 percent of the retail price of the car. If that figure didn't check, students should come see us for clarification. We made a note to teach multiplying by decimals later in the year so that students could investigate just what the calculator does when you use the percent key.

Lesson 16: Graph Your Budget

Materials

- **Make a Pie Graph from a Bar Graph,** S-24
- **Mental Math Warm-Up/Compatible Decimals•1,** page 127
- centimeter graph paper
- monthly budget from previous lesson
- colored markers or crayons
- overhead transparency
- overhead projector
- tape
- scissors
- rulers
- blank paper
- calculator

Advance Preparation

Try this project ahead of time. Make two copies of your bar graph so you can cut, tape, and form a circle with one graph for a class display. Leave the other graph intact.

Prepare a transparency of **Mental Math Warm-Up**, page 127.

Make a copy of **Make a Pie Graph from a Bar Graph**, S-24, for each student.

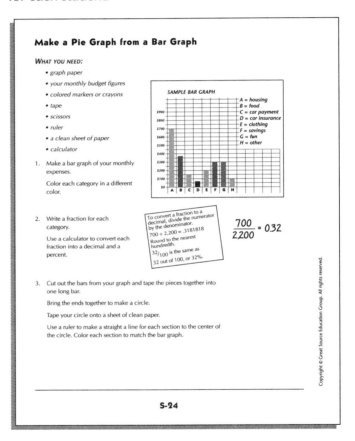

Objectives

- to represent data using a bar graph
- to make a pie graph from the same data

Getting Started

Demonstrate the project by displaying the bar graph you have made from your sample budget. Then show how to cut the bars, tape them together into a large strip, and tape the end of the strip to the front to get a circle. Place this circle on a piece of paper to divide the circle into the correct proportions.

Display a transparency of **Mental Math Warm-Up**, page 127, and complete it with the students.

Graph Your Budget

BAR GRAPH: Have students complete **Make a Pie Graph from a Bar Graph**, S-24. Ask for ideas on a scale for the Y-axis. (Different incomes might require different scales.) On the X-axis, students will label each category such as housing, food, and car payment. Students will color each bar a different color.

CIRCLE GRAPH: Have students cut their bar graphs into strips and create their circles. Have them label each section of the pie with colors that correspond to their bar graphs.

Wrapping Up

Compare graphs after everyone has finished. Discuss whether people in different occupations spend the same proportions of their income on the necessities of life. Have students put the graphs in their project folders.

Extension/Homework

Have students create a pie graph using a compass with degrees. To find out degrees for each category, students should compute the percentage of each category; then multiply that percent by 360 to find out the number of degrees in each arc of the circle graph. (For example, housing might cost 34 percent of the monthly total. A 34-percent category translates into a 122-degree arc.)

For one student's careful explanation, see page 96.

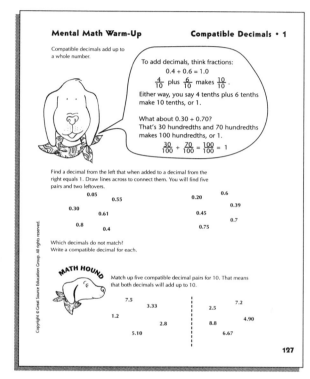

Mental Math Answer Key
Adding to 1:
  0.55 + 0.45
  0.61 + 0.39
  0.4 + 0.6
  0.8 + 0.20
  0.30 + 0.7
Leftovers: 0.05, 0.75
Compatibles: 0.05 + 0.95
  0.75 + 0.25

Five Compatible Pairs:
  7.5 + 2.5
  3.33 + 6.67
  2.8 + 7.2
  5.10 + 4.90
  1.2 + 8.8

Section 5 • Lesson 16

Lesson 17 — Car Buyer's Project
Phase III

Materials

- **Mental Math Warm-Up/Compatible Decimals • 2,** page 128
- **Car Buyer's Project • Phase III,** S-25
- **Resale Worksheet,** S-26
- **Car Buyer's Loan Worksheet** from earlier lesson
- calculators
- overhead transparency
- overhead projector

For **Extension/Homework:**

- Blue Book

Advance Preparation

Make transparencies of the **Car Buyer's Project • Phase III,** S-25, and **Resale Worksheet,** S-26, to demonstrate the activity. In addition, make copies of these pages for student use.

Prepare a transparency of **Mental Math Warm-Up,** page 128.

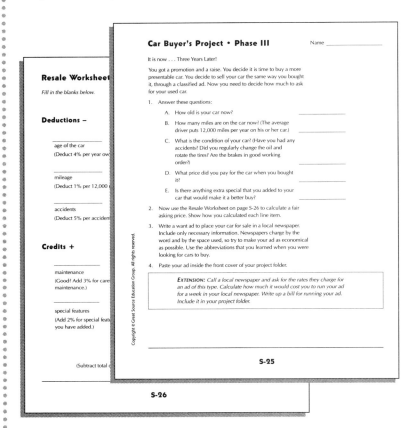

86 Using Fractions, Decimals, and Percent

Objectives

- to use information from an advertisement
- to create a car ad
- to apply concepts of rates in a real-world setting
- to apply decimal concepts in a real-world setting

Getting Started

Present the following scenario to the students:

> Three years after I bought my car, I got a promotion and a raise and decided that it was time to upgrade my car. I decided to talk to someone who really knew a lot about selling and buying cars. Here are all the tips I got to help me figure out how to price my used car.

Have students refer to their copies of **Car Buyer's Project • Phase III,** S-25, as you display the transparency.

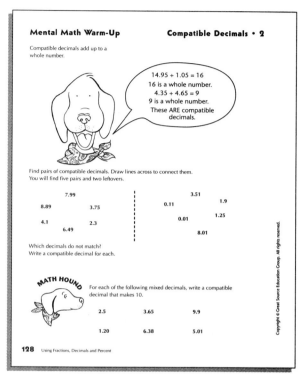

Then present sample resale data, demonstrating how to use the **Resale Worksheet,** S-26. Discuss each calculation as described on page 89. Keep the example display for reference as students prepare their individual **Resale Worksheets.**

Display a transparency of **Mental Math Warm-Up,** page 128, and complete it with the students.

Car Buyer's Project • Phase III

Have students prepare a **Resale Worksheet** for their individual cars. Be sure students write the equations they used to calculate each line item.

Wrapping Up

Have volunteers share their ads with the class.

Extension/Homework

Have students research the value of their used car using the **Blue Book** (available in public libraries and at car dealerships). Have them compare their asking price with the range of asking prices in the **Blue Book.** Ask: "How good a deal is their car now?"

Mental Math Answer Key

Compatible Pairs:
   7.99 + 0.01   3.75 + 1.25
   6.49 + 3.51   4.1 + 1.9
   8.89 + 0.11
Leftovers: 2.3, 8.01
Compatibles: 2.3 + 4.7
            8.01 + 1.99

Adding to 10:
   2.5 + 7.5   3.65 + 6.35
   9.9 + 0.1   1.20 + 8.80
   6.38 + 3. 62   5.01 + 4.99

Section 5 • Lesson 17   **87**

What Really Happened

We found it useful to display a transparency of a sample **Car Buyer's Loan Worksheet,** page S-20. Then we discussed how to use the loan worksheet to find needed information for the **Resale Worksheet,** S-26. Using the overhead projector, the class helped fill out a sample **Resale Worksheet,** before students worked independently. It was helpful to write sample equations that students could use as models when they applied new data.

Use sample data, such as on the sheet (S-20) to the left. As you discuss how to fill out a **Resale Worksheet,** work with students to develop the equations needed to calculate each line item. See page 89 for details.

Students used calculators as they worked. Making sense of the equations was easier because they did not simultaneously have to complete tedious calculations with messy numbers. When filling out their own resale worksheets, some students had to be reminded to write down the equations they entered into their calculators.

Calculating the mileage deduction was confusing to some students, since this deduction involves working with large numbers in a multistep problem-solving situation. These students found it helpful to make a rates table to understand the calculation. (See sample **Resale Worksheet** on page 89.)

Some students kept a running total as they calculated each line item. Then, rather than totaling the deductions, they simply subtracted and added as appropriate to arrive at a reasonable asking price.

Sample Car Buyer's Loan Worksheet

Name: Michael

- Make: Plymouth
- Model: Voyager
- Year: 1991
- Mileage: 91k
- Options: V6, AC, AT, pwr wds
- Retail price: $9,500

Financing this car   Today's date: _____

- Retail price: $9,500
- Down payment (10%): 950
- Amount to finance: 8,550

11% interest rate — Today's interest rate times amount to finance: .11 × 8,550 = 940.50

- Total financed amount: 9,490.50

- Total monthly payment: $197.72
  = 9,490.50 ÷ 48 months

S-20

88 Using Fractions, Decimals, and Percent

Resale Worksheet
Line-by-Line Equations

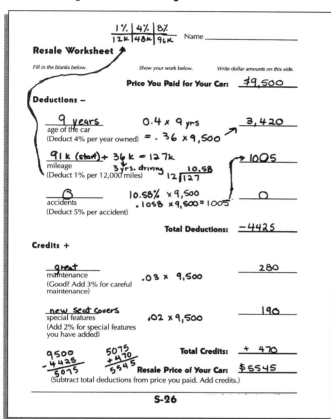

age of the car = *today's year minus model year x 0.04 x purchase price of car*

(Be sure students keep in mind that their car was not new when they bought it.)

mileage = *mileage when you bought it + (12,000 x number of years you owned it) x price you paid for the car*

mileage deduction = *(mileage ÷ 12,000) x 0.01*

accidents = *0.05 x price you paid for the car*

(Students generally say they have not had accidents—they want to ask as much as possible for their cars.)

maintenance = *0.03 x price you paid for car*

(Students generally take full maintenance value; you may want to ask them what they have done to maintain their cars.)

special features = *0.02 x price you paid for car*

(Students generally take credit for special features; we ask them to specify what they have done to add value to their car.)

Help students check their final resale price for reasonableness. Remind them that, after three years, they still owe one-fourth of the purchase price of their cars. The resale price should be at least that much.

Section 5 • Lesson 17   **89**

Lesson 18: STUDENT SELF-EVALUATION

Materials

- **Mental Math Warm-Up/Compatible Decimals • 3,** page 129
- **Car Buyer's Project • Self-Evaluation,** S-27
- **Car Buyer's Project • Grading Your Own Work,** S-28
- overhead projector
- overhead transparency

Advance Preparation

Prepare a transparency of **Mental Math Warm-Up**, page 129 to use with this lesson.

Make copies of **Car Buyer's Project • Self Evaluation** and **Car Buyer's Project Grading Your Own Work**, S-27 and S-28, for each student.

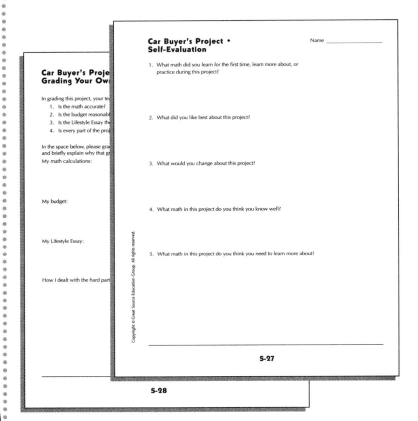

TEACHING TIP

ABOUT STUDENT SELF-ASSESSMENT

Before students evaluate their own work, you may want to have a class discussion about what makes for an excellent project. Work with the class to generate a list of assessment criteria and describe each to create benchmarks.

Using Fractions, Decimals, and Percent

Objectives
- to assess performance on a project
- to review learning

Getting Started
Tell students that today they will evaluate their own Car Buyer's Project and grade themselves on how well they did. Discuss the criteria listed on **Car Buyer's Project • Self-Evaluation,** S-27, and **Car Buyer's Project • Grading Your Own Work,** S-28.

If students have not yet created a project folder, have them do so using the guidelines from **Car Buyer's Project • Phase II • Organize Your Work,** S-23.

Student Self-Evaluation
Have students review their project folders, looking for specific examples in each evaluation category on S-27 and S-28. Circulate and coach as needed.

Wrapping Up
Ask students about their self-evaluation experience. Ask questions like:

"What do you think was the best thing about your work on this project?"

"What did you find hard?"

"What was most impressive in your project folder?"

"What advice would you have for someone who is just beginning the Car Buyer's Project?"

Then collect project folders.

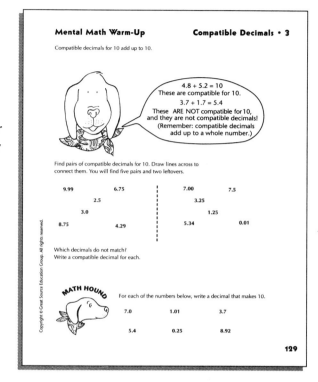

Mental Math Answer Key

Compatible Pairs:
9.99 + 0.01	6.75 + 3.25
2.5 + 7.5	3.0 + 7.00
8.75 + 1.25	

Leftovers: 4.29, 5.34
Compatibles:
4.29 + 5.71
5.34 + 4.66

Compatible to 10:
7.0 + 3.0	1.01 + 8.99
3.7 + 6.3	5.4 + 4.6
0.25 + 9.75	8.92 + 1.08

Car Buyer's Project • What Really Happened

Lauren's career as a brain surgeon allowed her to buy a luxury car. Her portfolio shows her at the wheel. Her worksheet accounted for a four-year loan.

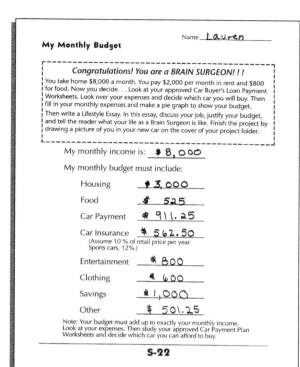

Lauren wrote a creative essay about her life as a brain surgeon.

"…After a hard day at work extracting brain tumors and experimenting with brain transplant research animals, I am very exhausted and stressed out. I therefore don't have much time or energy for food shopping or cooking dinner for myself. Because of this, I tend to eat out 3 to 4 times a week at only the best gourmet restaurants.

$911.25 worth of my paycheck goes to my car payments to pay off the money for my new Porsche. If you can believe it, the car insurance payments are almost as expensive as the car payments! $562.50!! A month!

Every month I spend $800 on entertainment. I enjoy going to movies, concerts, art galleries and even the ballet . . . ."

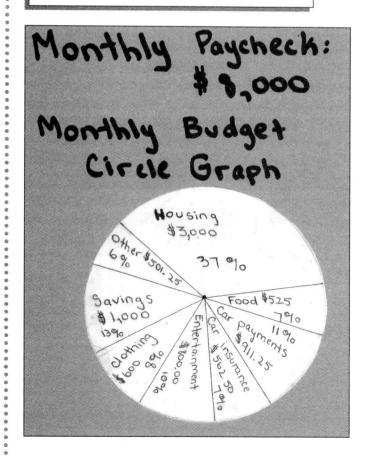

For his report, Michael became a teacher who drives a used red Plymouth Voyager. His essay shows an understanding of his budget as part of life.

My Life

All my life I've wanted to be a teacher in pre-K because I've always liked children. I'm happily married with two kids, a boy who is ten and a five-year-old girl. My daughter is in pre-K and she is in the class I teach. My son is in fourth grade and he plays basketball and baseball. I have a nice one story house with a big lawn. My monthly salary is $3000. I have a red Plymouth Voyager that is in good condition. Since I could not buy it all at once I'm buying it over a period of four years. I'm paying $197.72 per month and $95.00 per month for car insurance.

Since my job is working with children all day I need a lot of money for entertainment which comes out to be $475.00 per month. Each month I go to about two movies and a lot of fancy restaurants to just relax without kids around. I have $400.00 in clothing each month because for some reason when a kid spills paint or grape juice, it always lands on me ruining my clothes. Since I care about my children and their education so much, I put $132.28 in the bank every month. I am saving for them to go to college. Who knows, maybe one of them will become a supreme court judge or even president. Who knows, they could become both.

I have $500.00 a month for other things because some times little things come up. For instance, the other day I was driving on University Ave. I forgot that the speed limit is 25 MPH. Who knew a refrigerator on wheels could go so fast. Nevertheless I was written up for doing 35 MPH, which cost $85.00.

Michael's budget:

Take home $3,000 a month.

Housing	$900
Food	$300
Car Payment	$197.72
Car Insurance	$95
Entertainment	$475
Clothing	$400
Savings	$132.28
Other	$500
TOTAL	$3,000

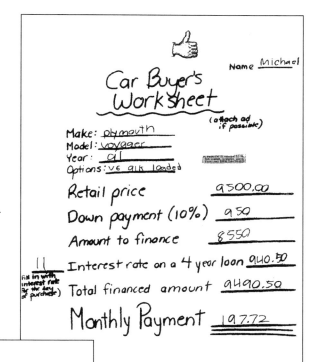

When Michael did this project, he figured on a four-year loan.

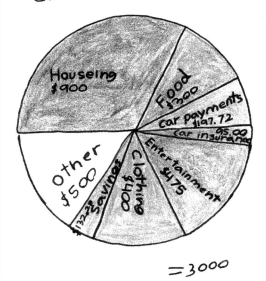

Section 5 • Lesson 18

Sharing Ideas and Strategies

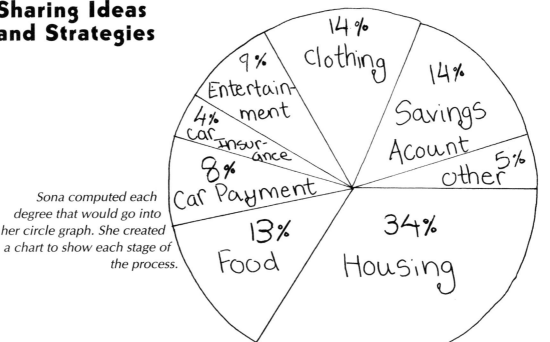

Sona computed each degree that would go into her circle graph. She created a chart to show each stage of the process.

	Decimal	Percent	Decimal × 360° to find degree
Housing	$\frac{750}{2200} = .34$	34%	.34 × 360 = 122°
Food	$\frac{275}{2200} = .13$	13%	.13 × 360 = 47°
Car P.	$\frac{174.15}{2200} = .08$	8%	.08 × 360 = 29°
Car I.	$\frac{86}{2200} = .04$	4%	.04 × 360 = 14°
Entertainment	$\frac{200}{2200} = .09$	9%	.09 × 360 = 32°
Clothes	$\frac{300}{2200} = .14$	14%	.14 × 360 = 50°
Savings	$\frac{300}{2200} = .14$	14%	.14 × 360 = 50°
Other	$\frac{114.85}{2200} = .05$	5%	.05 × 360 = 18°
	1.01	101%	362°

So I minused 2° from "Entertainment" (30°). Then that equaled a total of 360.

Using Fractions, Decimals, and Percent

THE STOCK MARKET PROJECT

SECTION 6

LESSON 19: TRACK TOOTHPASTE STOCK
          LITERATURE CONNECTION:
          THE TOOTHPASTE MILLIONAIRE
          BY JEAN MERRILL   **98**

LESSON 20: GRAPH YOUR STOCK   **100**

LESSON 21: DID YOUR STOCK GROW IN VALUE?   **102**

Lesson 19: TRACK TOOTHPASTE STOCK

Materials

- *The Toothpaste Millionaire* by Jean Merrill
- **Mental Math Warm-Up/Friendly Fractions • 1,** page 130
- **Toothpaste Shareholder's Math 1,** S-29
- **Toothpaste Shareholder's Math-2,** S-30
- chart paper
- markers
- calculators (optional)
- overhead projector
- overhead transparency

Advance Preparation

Prepare a transparency of **Mental Math Warm-up**, page 130, to use with this lesson.

Make copies of **Toothpaste Shareholder's Math 1** and **2**, S-29 and S-30, for each student.

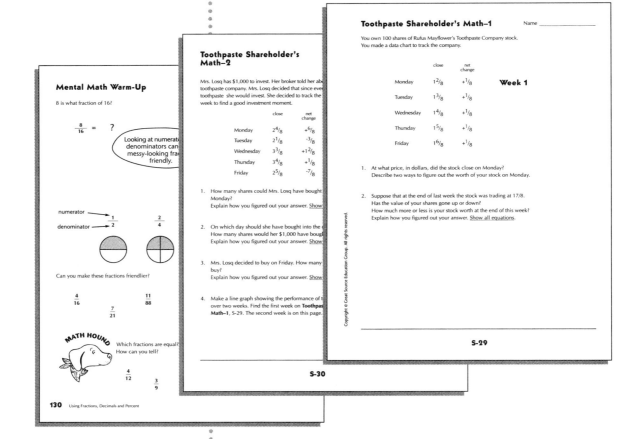

Objectives
- to apply rate formulas to determine the value of a stock
- to make a line graph

Getting Started
Explain that Rufus Mayflower's Toothpaste Company has gone public and has issued stock. Its price is $1\frac{2}{8}$. Ask students how much that is in dollars and cents.

Have students help you create a display chart that transfers eighths to decimal amounts. It might look like:

$\frac{1}{8}$ of a dollar is $0.125 or 12.5¢
$\frac{2}{8}$ of a dollar is $0.25 or 25¢
$\frac{3}{8}$ of a dollar is $0.375 or 37.5¢
$\frac{4}{8}$ of a dollar is $0.50 or 50¢
$\frac{5}{8}$ of a dollar is $0.625 or 62.5¢
$\frac{6}{8}$ of a dollar is $0.75 or 75¢
$\frac{7}{8}$ of a dollar is $0.875 or 87.5¢
$\frac{8}{8}$ of a dollar is $1.00 or 100¢

Display a transparency of **Mental Math Warm-Up**, page 130, and complete it with the students.

Track Toothpaste Stock
Distribute S-29 and S-30. Have students work on their equations. Before students create graphs with their data, model the process for them. Explain that their goal is to show changes in the price of their stock. Elicit that to show small changes in data, you need to choose the right scale for the Y-axis.

Create two line graphs on the board. On one, make a scale from 1 to 10 with intervals of 1. On the other Y-axis, make a scale from 1 to $3\frac{1}{2}$ with intervals of $\frac{1}{4}$. Have volunteers graph the data on the two graphs. Then ask students to compare the graphs. Ask for ideas about how to choose the better range on the Y-axis for these data.

Wrapping Up
Compare student graphs. Are they all the same?

Extension/Homework
Have students copy the eighths-to-decimals chart. Ask them to write about patterns they observe in this chart.

Mental Math Answer Key

Friendly Fractions:

$\frac{4}{16} = \frac{1}{4}$ $\frac{7}{21} = \frac{1}{3}$

$\frac{11}{88} = \frac{1}{8}$ $\frac{13}{39} = \frac{1}{3}$

$\frac{5}{20} = \frac{1}{4}$ $\frac{8}{32} = \frac{1}{4}$

Equal Fractions:

$\frac{4}{12}$, $\frac{3}{9}$, $\frac{12}{36}$, $\frac{5}{15}$ are equal fractions.

You can tell because they can be reduced to $\frac{1}{3}$.

$\frac{5}{20}$ and $\frac{15}{60}$ are equal fractions.

You can tell because they can be reduced to $\frac{1}{4}$.

LITERATURE CONNECTION

The Toothpaste Millionaire by Jean Merrill

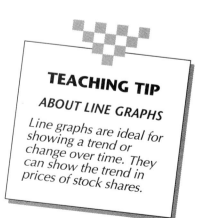

TEACHING TIP

ABOUT LINE GRAPHS

Line graphs are ideal for showing a trend or change over time. They can show the trend in prices of stock shares.

Lesson 20: GRAPH YOUR STOCK

Materials
- completed **Stock Recording Sheet**, S-3
- **Did Your Stock Grow in Value?**, S-31
- graph paper
- rulers
- pencils
- markers

For **Extensions/ Homework:**
- **Mental Math Warm-Up/ Friendly Fractions**
  - **2**, page 131

Advance Preparation

Make copies of **Did Your Stock Grow in Value?**, S-31, for student use. Consider the number of entries your students made on their recording sheets (S-3) as you provide graph paper for this project. If they have 20 entries, make sure the paper is at least 20 squares wide. Copies of the graph paper on page 117 would work if the page is turned.

As you are planning this lesson, keep in mind that students will do the lower half of page S-31, the **Invest $1,000** problem, during a later class.

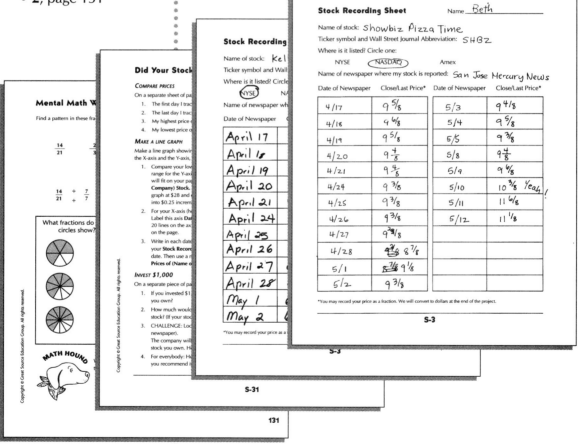

100 Using Fractions, Decimals, and Percent

Objectives

- to create a line graph from data
- to choose intervals that will create a scale to indicate movement

Getting Started

Explain that students will be graphing their personal stocks just as they graphed the toothpaste stock. Ask students to look at the stock data they have collected over the last month. Have them note the highest and lowest prices in their data. Review that $52\frac{1}{4}$ represents $52.25 on a stock price table.

Display student recording sheets. Students' stocks will have different ranges of high and low prices. Ask for ideas on what range to write on the vertical axis. Also discuss how to set up the data on the page. If students have 20 days' worth of data, they will have to have 20 dates listed on their X-axis.

Graph Your Stock

Distribute S-31, and have students refer to the guidelines on graphing stock value. As students work on graphing their stocks, circulate and observe. Make sure line graphs have both axes labeled with appropriate titles.

Wrapping Up

Compare some line graphs. Display some that indicate upward movement and others that show downward movement. Ask students which type of movement most stockholders would prefer.

Discuss challenges students faced as they made their graphs. (Some students may have had very little change to work with.)

Extensions/Homework

Have students create a poster or brochure that tells about the company they invested in. Their poster should include a description of the company and its products, a graph showing their stock's performance, a paragraph about their stock performance as shown on their line graph, and the answer to this question: "Did you make money?"

Distribute **Mental Math Warm-Up/Friendly Fractions •2**, page 131 to the students. Review their work.

Mental Math Answer Key

Friendly Fractions:
Numbers 1, 2, 5, and 6 = $\frac{1}{2}$.
Numbers 3 and 4 = $\frac{1}{3}$.

$\frac{6}{11} + \frac{5}{9}$ will add up to more than 1 because each is greater than $\frac{1}{2}$.

Each of the three pie graphs is equal to $\frac{2}{3}$.

Lesson 21 — Did Your Stock Grow in Value?

Materials

- **Stock Recording Sheet,** S-3, filled with student data from newspapers
- **Did Your Stock Grow in Value?,** S-31
- **Mental Math Warm-Up/Estimating Fractions,** page 132
- newspaper stock tables
- construction paper and markers
- overhead projector
- overhead transparency

Advance Preparation

Prepare a transparency of **Mental Math Warm-Up**, page 132, to use with this lesson.

Make a copy of **Did Your Stock Grow in Value?**, S-31, for each student.

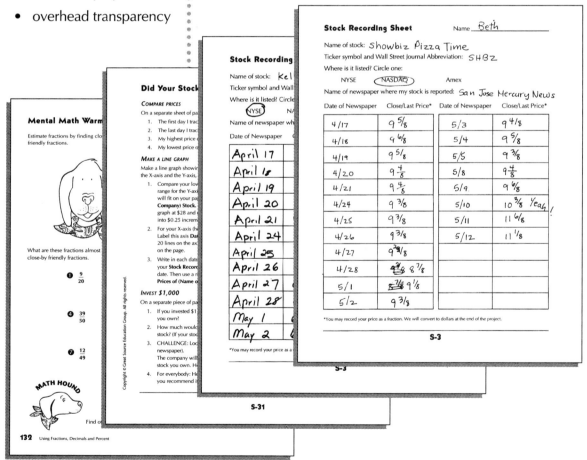

102 Using Fractions, Decimals, and Percent

Objectives
- to apply rate formulas to determine value of a stock
- to evaluate an investment

Getting Started

Explain to students that they will pretend that they each had $1,000 to invest the first day they started recording their stock data. Point out that the class was lucky enough to find a stockbroker who charged no sales commission. (In the real world, this wouldn't happen, but it keeps the math simple.) Tell students they will compare the starting price and finish price of their stock.

Display a transparency of **Mental Math Warm-Up**, page 132, and complete it with the students.

Did Your Stock Grow in Value?

Have students follow the instructions on the lower half of S-31. As students work, circulate and observe. If students have a stock that did not change in value, show them how to look up the dividend in the newspaper stock market table. Explain that sometimes people buy stocks because the stock will pay them money, called a *dividend*. (On page S-2, students can see that IBM pays a dividend of $1.00 per share per year.)

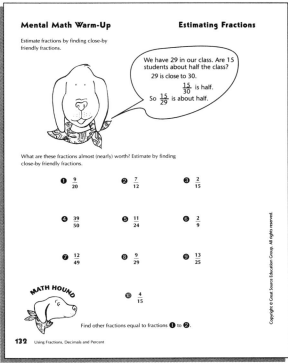

Wrapping Up

Ask students for ideas on why a company prospers. Discuss the challenges faced by the business in ***The Toothpaste Millionaire***.

Review the Law of Supply and Demand. (If there are more buyers for a limited number of stock shares, the price will go up. If there are fewer buyers, the price will go down.)

Invite students to evaluate their companies as investments. Ask: "Did they grow in value? Did they pay a dividend?" Encourage students to suggest factors that might affect a company's prosperity and the value of its stock.

Write About Math: Have students write to the following prompt in their math journal:

"What three tips would you give to a student who is just beginning the Stock Market Project?"

Mental Math Answer Key
Close-by Estimates:
1. $\frac{1}{2}$ 2. $\frac{1}{2}$ 3. $\frac{1}{5}$
4. $\frac{1}{4}$ 5. $\frac{1}{2}$ 6. $\frac{1}{3}$
7. $\frac{1}{4}$ 8. $\frac{1}{3}$ 9. $\frac{1}{2}$
10. $\frac{1}{3}$

Equal Fractions:
1. $\frac{45}{100}$ 2. $\frac{21}{36}$ 3. $\frac{6}{45}$
4. $\frac{78}{100}$ 5. $\frac{22}{48}$ 6. $\frac{6}{27}$
7. $\frac{24}{98}$ 8. $\frac{18}{58}$ 9. $\frac{26}{50}$
10. $\frac{16}{60}$

Section 6 • Lesson 21 **103**

Veterans of the Stock Market Project offered advice to students who are just starting.

Irene, above, suggested using what you already know about graphs. Marcus, right, offered advice on a crucial math skill.

What Really Happened

> Reuse what you already know about graphs.

> Learn how to turn fractions into decimals.

> Its good to do research and know something about the company you're going to invest money in. Send away for information about your company to help you write the essay for the poster.

Irene also offered planning tips, advising that you send away early for information about your company. Below, Marc suggested the key to making the project interesting.

> Don't get frustrated in the beginning when you don't understand how to read the stock pages.
>
> Pick a stock that you are interested in so the project's interesting.

WHAT DID WE LEARN?

SECTION 7

LESSON 22: MINI-PORTFOLIO— ASSESSMENT 3   **106**

 # MINI-PORTFOLIO

Materials
- **Mini-Portfolio,** S-32
- previous student work

Advance Preparation
Make a copy of **Mini-Portfolio,** S-32, for each student.

Mini-Portfolio   Name _____   Date _____

WHAT YOU NEED:
- your completed Ants' Picnic worksheet
- activity sheets for "Picturing Decimals, Fractions, and Percent"
- game recording sheets
- budgets from the Car Buyer's Project
- graph from the Stock Market Project
- "What I Already Know About Decimals" essay

1. Review the teacher's comments on your Ants' Picnic worksheet. Respond to the questions or suggestions. Then write a short paragraph describing what you learned from this activity.

2. Make a list of all the games, worksheets and activities you completed in this unit. Rate the activities from your favorite to your least favorite.

   Then write a short paragraph (at least three sentences) to explain what you learned from one of these activities.

3. Reread your essay, "Write About Decimals" and then think about what you know now. Describe three new things that you learned.

4. Respond to one of the following:

   One really amazing thing about decimals is . . .

   or

   With decimals, I think I'll need to learn more about . . .

   (As you respond, think about some of these questions: Did you learn new things that surprised you? What connections do you see between decimals, fractions, and percent? Does anything about decimals still confuse you? What else do you think you'll need to understand about decimals to be really confident?)

EXTRA CHALLENGE:

Use a calculator to solve these multiplication problems. Then explain why each answer makes sense. (HINT: You may find it helpful to think about fractions that are equal to some of these decimals.)

   a. 4.12 × .25   b.   4.12 × 2.5

How would you solve these problems without a calculator?

S-32

Objectives

- to help students' assess their own learning
- to review activities related to using decimals, fractions, and percentages

Getting Started

Have students gather together the work done over the past six weeks. Explain that they will create a mini-portfolio following the instructions on S-32.

Mini-Portfolio

Circulate and observe as students work.

Wrapping Up

Display the class chart you and your students created in the first lesson, **Write About Decimals.** Review the statements that students made the first day of class. Ask: "Has anyone changed his or her mind about any statements made one month ago?"

Then have students discuss the essay responses on S-32 by asking:

"What did you list as a really amazing thing about decimals?"

"What more do you feel you need to learn about decimals?"

What Really Happened

> Nate
>
> I learned that if you have one number to the right of the decimal like .5 the .5 means tenth and not oneth. I also learned how to read realy tiny numbers quickly like .135789105. Another thing I learned was how to read numbers to the negetive power like 10-4.

> I learned lots from decimal war. I leared how to read decimals better. I also saw how the same things could be writen many different ways.

Above, Nate demonstrated his understanding of place value.

At right, Thomas described a "Decimal War," a game similar to Comparing and Ordering Decimals. His insight, that the same thing could be written many different ways, will prepare him for algebra.

> 1. I know that if it is one thousandth instead of seeing tree zeros in the number like it would be if it was a hole number you would see one less zero.
>
> 2. I learned the decmils are just like numbers and are easy to work with once you figure it out.
>
> 3. And I learned that the numbers are said the sam except you add a th's if it was a decimal.

> Three new things I learned about decimals are.... 1) That you have to use a calculator on most decimal probs to be accurate.
> 2) I learned what a thousandth looks like in a paper brownie.
> 3) 10 to the minus something can also be expressed as a decimal.

Above, Lauren noted the connection between exponents and decimals.

Right, Ryo described his emerging understanding of place value.

> The decimel devides the hole numbers from the tenths and hundreths thats what I learned about the decimel because I didnt know there was a tenth or hundreth.

> I learned that 2.5 is the same as 2.50. I also learned how to read decimals beter.

To the left, Andre described two ways to express the same number.

Below, Amber offered a general overview showing the connection between decimals and fractions.

> Some new things that I learned are decimals can be written in many different forms, decimals can be multiplyed by each other, decimals are fractions of whole numbers, decimals can bee shown by coloring in squares that are inside a big square.

> One really weird thing about decimals is why do they exsist why don't we just use fractions they're much easier to read and write.

> One really weird thing about decimals is even though the smallest place is right after the decimal that's where you start to read a decimal number.

> One really weird thing that I find about decimals is that when you are talking about large numbers such as a trillion, when you get into smaller numbers you add a ths on the end of the real place value. For instince one trillionth.

> One really weird thing I learned about decimals is that there is also infinity behind a decimal! (there is infinity in decimals too!)

"One really weird thing about decimals is…" Students relished finishing this question. David, top, thought decimals were so difficult to use, it was amazing they existed. Louise, David, Sona, and Lauren discussed reading decimals, large and small numbers, and infinite possibilities in decimals.

TEACHER RESOURCES

SECTION 8

STUDENT EVALUATION CHECKLISTS	**112**
SELECTED U.S. STOCKS	**114**
CENTIMETER GRAPH PAPER	**117**
GET OFF THE FIELD! (GAME BOARD)	**118**
SAMPLE CAR AD	**119**
THE VIDEO STORE CLERK'S BUDGET	**120**
CAREER DESCRIPTIONS—1	**121**
CAREER DESCRIPTIONS—2	**122**
CAREER DESCRIPTIONS—3	**123**
CAREER DESCRIPTIONS—4	**124**
MENTAL MATH WARM-UPS	**125**
BIBLIOGRAPHY	**133**
INDEX	**133**

Evaluation Checklist

Student											
Decimal Concepts											
Reads and writes decimals through millionths											
Compares and orders decimals through millionths											
Relates decimals to fractions and percent											
Finds simple percents of a number											
Estimates 10 percent											
Estimates 15 percent											
Converts fractional stock listings to dollar values											
Correctly reads aloud decimals and mixed numbers											
Devises appropriate scales for graphs and time lines											
Multiplies by 1,000											
Divides by 1,000											
Rounds to appropriate place value											

Evaluation Checklist

Student

Strategy Development

Uses multiple representations for concepts										
Creates/uses visual or pictorial models										
Uses calculator proficiently										
Can explain mental math strategies										
Demonstrates proficiency with more than one strategy										
Consciously builds on prior knowledge										

Communication Skills

Asks relevant questions										
Restates problems clearly										
Listens to others										
Participates in discussion										
Organizes data on charts										
Represents situations with graphs										
Writes clear explanations										

SELECTED U.S. STOCKS–1

Company Name	Address	Ticker Symbol/ WSJ Abbrev.	Where*
Apparel			
Gap Inc.	1 Harrison St., San Francisco, CA 94105-1602	GPS/Gap	NYSE
Levi Strauss Assoc. Inc.	1155 Battery St., San Francisco, CA 94111-1256		NYSE
Oshkosh B'Gosh Inc.	112 Otter Ave., Oshkosh, WI 54901-5067	GOSHA/OshBA	NASDAQ
Ross Stores Inc.	8333 Central Ave., Newark, CA 94560-3440	ROST/RossStr	NASDAQ
Athletic Shoes			
L.A. Gear Inc.	2850 Ocean Park Blvd., Santa Monica, CA 90405-2936	LA/LA Gear	NYSE
Nike Inc.	1 SW Bowerman Dr., Beaverton, OR 97005-6453	NKE/NikeB	NYSE
Reebok International Ltd.	100 Technology Center Dr., Stoughton, MA 02072-4702	RBK/Reebok	NYSE
Biotechnology and Medical Products			
Coherent Inc.	5100 Patrick Henry Dr., Santa Clara, CA 95054-1112	COHR/Cohernt	NASDAQ
Genentech	460 Point San Bruno Blvd., So.San Francisco, CA 94080-4990	GNE/Genentec	NYSE
Nellcor Inc.	4280 Hacienda Dr., Pleasanton, CA 94588-2719	Nell/Nellcor	NASDAQ
Comics and Cards			
Marvel Entertainment Grp.	387 Park Ave. S, 12th Fl., New York, NY 10016-8810	MRV/Marvel	NYSE
Score Board Inc.	1951 Old Cuthbert Rd., Cherry Hill, NJ 08034-1417	BSBL/ScoreBd	NASDAQ
Communications			
AirTouch Communications Corp.	425 Market St., 36th Fl., San Francisco, CA 94105-2406	ATI/AirTouch	NYSE
AT &T Corp.	32 Ave. of the Americas, New York, NY 10013-2473	T/AT&T	NYSE
MCI Communications Corp.	1801 Pennsylvania Ave. NW, Washington, DC 20006-3606	MCI/MCI	NASDAQ
Sprint Corp.	2330 Shawnee Mission Pkwy., Shawnee Mission, KS 66205-2005	FON/Sprint	NYSE
Computers and Software			
Adobe Systems Inc.	1585 Charleston Rd., Mtn. View, CA 94043-1225	ADBE/AdobeSy	NASDAQ
Apple Computer Inc.	20525 Mariani Ave., Cupertino, CA 95014-6202	AAPL/AppleC	NASDAQ
Broderbund Software Inc.	500 Redwood Blvd., Novato, CA 94947-6921	BROD/BrodSft	NASDAQ
Compaq Computer Corp.	20555 Sh 249, Houston, TX 77070	CPQ/Compaq	NYSE
Dell Computer Corp.	9505 Arboretum Blvd., Austin, TX 78759-7299	DELL/DellCpt	NASDAQ
Hewlett-Packard Co. Inc.	3000 Hanover St., Palo Alto, CA 94304-1181	HWP/HewlPk	NYSE
International Business Machines Corp.(IBM)	Old Orchard Rd., Armonk, NY 10504	IBM/IBM	NYSE
Intuit Inc.	66 Willow Place, Menlo Park, CA 94025-3601	INTU/Intuit	NASDAQ
Microsoft Corp.	1 Microsoft Way, Redmond, WA 98052-8300	MSFT/Microsoft	NASDAQ
Xerox Corp.	800 Long Ridge Rd., Stamford, CT 06902-1227	XRX/Xerox	NYSE

*Key to Stock Exchanges or Markets (where stock is listed)

NYSE	*New York Stock Exchange*
AMEX	*American Stock Exchange*
NASDAQ	*National Association of Security Dealers Automated Quotation System*

SELECTED U.S. STOCKS-2

Company Name	Address	Ticker Symbol/ WSJ Abbrev.	Where*
Electronics			
Circuit City Stores Inc.	9950 Maryland Dr., Richmond, VA 23233-1464	CC/CirCity	NYSE
Eastman Kodak Co. Inc.	343 State St., Rochester, NY 14650-0001	EK/EKodak	NYSE
Gametek	2999 NE 191st St., Ste 500, Miami, FL 33180-3117	GAME/Gametek	NASDAQ
Food Products			
Campbell Soup	Campbell Place, Camden, NJ 08103	CPB/CampSp	NYSE
Chiquita Brands Intl. Inc.	250 E. 5th St., Cincinnati, OH 45202-4103	CQB/Chiquita	NYSE
Coca Cola Co. Inc.	1 Coca Cola Plaza NW, Atlanta, GA 30313-2499	KO/CocaCl	NYSE
Dole Food Co. Inc.	31355 Oak Crest Dr., Thousand Oaks, CA 91361-4633	DOL/Dole	NYSE
Hershey Foods Corp.	100 Crystal A Drive, Hershey, PA 17033-0810	HSY/Hershey	NYSE
Kellogg Co. Inc.	1 Kellogg Square, Battle Creek, MI 49017-3599	K/Kellogg	NYSE
Pepsico Inc.	Anderson Hill Rd., Purchase, NY 10577	PEP/PepsiCo	NYSE
Quaker Oats Co. Inc.	321 N. Clark St., Chicago, IL 60610-4714	OAT/QuakrOat	NYSE
RJR Nabisco Holdings Corp.	1301 Ave. of the Americas, New York, NY 10019-6022`	RN/RJRNab	NYSE
Sara Lee Corp.	3-1st National Place, Chicago, IL 60602	SLE/SaraLee	NYSE
Smucker JM Co., The	Strawberry Lane, Orrville, OH 44667	SJM.A/Smckr B	NYSE
Tootsie Roll Industries Inc.	7401 S. Cicero Ave., Chicago, IL 60629-5885	TR/TootsieR	NYSE
Wrigley Wm. Jr. Co. Inc.	410 N. Michigan Ave., Chicago, IL 60611-4288	WWY/Wrigley	NYSE
Food Servers			
El Chico Restaurants Inc.	12200 N. Stemmons Fwy., Dallas, TX 75234-5877	ELCH/ElChico	NASDAQ
IHOP Corp.	525 N. Brand Blvd., Glendale, CA 91203-1903	IHOP/IHOPCp	NASDAQ
McDonald's Corp.	McDonald's Plaza, Hinsdale, IL 60521	MCD/McDnlds	NYSE
Showbiz Pizza Time Inc.	4441 W. Airport Fwy, Irving, TX 75062-5834	SHBZ/Showbiz	NASDAQ
Sizzler Intl. Inc.	12655 W. Jefferson Blvd., Los Angeles, CA 90066-7008	SZ/Sizzler	NYSE
TCBY Enterprises Inc.	425 W. Capitol Ave., Little Rock, AR 72201-3439	TBY/TCBY	NYSE
Wendy's Intl. Inc.	4288 W. Dublin Granville Rd., Dublin, OH 43017-2093	WEN/Wendys	NYSE
Retailers/Wholesalers			
JCPenney Co. Inc.	6501 Legacy Dr., Plano, TX 75024-3612`	JCP/Penney	NYSE
KMart Corp.	3100 W. Big Beaver Rd., Troy, MI 48084-3163	KM/K mart	NYSE
Natural Wonders Inc.	4209 Technology Dr., Fremont, CA 94538-6339	NATW/NatWndr	NASDAQ
Price/Costco	10809 120th Ave. NE, Kirkland, WA 98033-5024	PCCW/PriceCst	NASDAQ
Sears Roebuck & Co.	Sears Tower, Chicago, IL 60606	S/Sears	NYSE
Toys "R" Us Inc.	461 From Rd., Paramus, NJ 07652-3526	TOY/ToyRU	NYSE
WalMart Stores	705 SW 8th St., Bentonville, AR 72712-6209	WMT/WalMart	NYSE

*Key to Stock Exchanges or Markets (where stock is listed)

NYSE	New York Stock Exchange
AMEX	American Stock Exchange
NASDAQ	National Association of Security Dealers Automated Quotation System

SELECTED U.S. STOCKS–3

Company Name	Address	Ticker Symbol/ WSJ Abbrev.	Where*
Services & Transportation			
Alaska Air Group Inc.	19300 Pacific Hwy. S., Seattle, WA 98188-5303	ALK/AlskAir	NYSE
American Express Co. Inc.	American Express Tower, New York, NY 10285	AXP/AmExp	NYSE
Continental Airlines Inc.	2929 Allen Pky., Ste. 1100, Houston, TX 77019-2197	CAI.A/CtlAir	NYSE
Delta Air Lines Inc.	Hartsfield Intl. Airport, Atlanta, GA 30320	DAL/DeltaAir	NYSE
Federal Express Corp.	2005 Corporate Ave., Memphis, TN 38132-1796	FDX/FedExp	NYSE
Hilton Hotels Corp.	9336 Civic Center Dr., Beverly Hills, CA 90210-3604	HLT/Hilton	NYSE
Sports/Outdoor Recreation			
Coleman Co. Inc.	250 N. St. Francis St., Wichita, KS 67202-2610	CLN/Colemn	NYSE
Gymboree Corp.	700 Airport Blvd., Ste 200, Burlingame, CA 94010-1931	GYMB/Gymbree	NASDAQ
Harley-Davidson Inc.	3700 W. Juneau Ave., Milwaukee, WI 53208-2865	HDI/HarleyD	NYSE
Huffy Corp.	7701 Byers Rd., Miamisburg, OH 45342-3657	HUF/Huffy	NYSE
Rawlings Sporting Goods Co. Inc.	1859 Intertech Dr., Fenton, MO 63026-1906	RAWL/Rawling	NASDAQ
Toy Manufacturers			
Galoob Lewis Toys Inc.	500 Forbes Blvd., So. San Francisco, CA 94080-2092	GAL/Galoob	NYSE
Hasbro Inc.	1027 Newport Ave., Pawtucket, RI 02861-2539	HAS/Hasbro	AMEX
Mattel Inc.	333 Continental Blvd., El Segundo, CA 90245-5032	MAT/Mattel	NYSE
Tyco Toys Inc.	6000 Midlantic Dr., Mount Laurel, NJ 08054-1516	TTI/TycoToy	NYSE
TV/Movies			
CBS Inc.	51 W. 52nd St., New York, NY 10019-6188	West	NYSE
Disney (Walt) Co. Inc.	500 S. Buena Vista St., Burbank, CA 91521-0001	DIS/Disney	NYSE
Time-Warner Inc.	75 Rockefeller Plaza, New York, NY 10019-6908	TWX/TimeWa	NYSE
Twentieth Century Fox Inc.	10201 W. Pico Blvd, Los Angeles, CA 90064-2606	TW/20CentInd	NYSE
Miscellaneous			
Exxon Corp.	225 Lyndon B. Johnson Fwy, Irving, Tx 75063-3704	Exxon	NYSE
Ford Motor Co.	American Rd., Dearborn, MI 48121	FordM/Ford Motor	NYSE
General Motors Corp.	3044 W. Grand Blvd., Detroit, MI 48202-3080	GMH/GnMotr	NYSE
Lockheed Martin	4500 Park Granada, Calabasas, CA 91302-1613	LMT/LockhdM	NYSE

NOTE: Each newspaper uses its own abbreviated listing for each stock, but students should be able to recognize and identify their stock listing if they study the three- or four-letter ticker symbol and the *Wall Street Journal* abbreviation. *This list was researched in 1995; have students update as needed.*

*Key to Stock Exchanges or Markets (where stock is listed)

NYSE	*New York Stock Exchange*
AMEX	*American Stock Exchange*
NASDAQ	*National Association of Security Dealers Automated Quotation System*

Using Fractions, Decimals and Percent

Get Off the Field!

Player 1 | Player 2 | Player 3 | Player 4

Cut out the oval Player Cards and the square game cards.

Go to 1,000 place.	Divide your place by 100.
Move three places larger.	÷ 10
Move three places smaller.	× 10,000
Multiply your place by 1,000,000.	÷ 100
× 100	Go to ten thousandths place.

Want more game cards? Write your own instructions on square cards.

Game Board

Get Off the Field!

- Millions
- Hundred Thousands
- Ten Thousands
- Thousands
- Hundreds
- Tens
- Ones — Start Here.
- Tenths
- Hundredths
- Thousandths
- Ten Thousandths
- Hundred Thousandths
- Millionths — Get Off the Field!

118 Using Fractions, Decimals and Percent

ACURA INTEGRA LS SPECIAL '91: 5-speed, blk, 42K, xclnt cond, AC/cruise control. $12,500/bo. (999)555-1111

BRONCO '92: 29K MI. $18,800. **ACURA INTEGRA RS '90:** 4-dr, red, A/C, 47K mi $8,900/BO. Both excellent cond. 555-2222 Chuck, eves.

CADILLAC SEDANVILLE '90: Fully loaded, good condition. $6,000. (000)999-0000. Ask for Louie.

CHEVY SPRINT '85: 5-spd, 68K, orig ownr, $800. (555)999-9999

HONDA ACCORD LX '80: 2-dr, htchbk, 5-spd, AM/FM cass, A/C, runs good.$1500/b.o. (999)555-0000

MERCEDES 560SEL '87: lt gry/bg, orig ownr, AT, CD, snrf. All serv rec.Loaded.$23K OBO (999)000-5555

The Video Store Clerk's Budget

> **Congratulations! You are a VIDEO STORE CLERK!!!**
>
> You take home $1,200 a month. You pay $320 per month in rent and $240 for food. Now you decide... Look at your approved Car Buyer's Loan Payment worksheets. Look over your expenses and decide which car you will buy. Next, fill in your monthly expenses and make a pie graph to show your budget.
>
> Then write a Lifestyle Essay. In this essay, discuss your job, justify your budget, and tell the reader what your life as a Video Store Clerk is like. Finish the project by drawing a picture of you in your new car on the cover of your project folder.

Your monthly income is:

Your monthly budget must include:

Housing _____

Food _____

Car Payment _____

Car Insurance _____
(Assume 10 % of retail price per year. Sports cars, 12%.)

Entertainment _____

Clothing _____

Savings _____

Other _____

NOTE: Your budget must add up to exactly your monthly income.

Career Descriptions–1

Congratulations! You are a TEACHER!!!

You take home $3,000 a month. You pay $600 per month in rent and $300 for food. Now you decide. . . Look at your approved Car Buyer's Loan Payment worksheets. Look over your expenses and decide which car you will buy. Next, fill in your monthly expenses and make a pie graph to show your budget.

Then write a Lifestyle Essay. In this essay, discuss your job, justify your budget, and tell the reader what your life as a Teacher is like. Finish the project by drawing a picture of you in your new car on the cover of your project folder.

Congratulations! You are a LAWYER!!!

You take home $5,000 a month. You pay $2,000 per month in rent and $500 for food. Now you decide. . . Look at your approved Car Buyer's Loan Payment worksheets. Look over your expenses and decide which car you will buy. Next, fill in your monthly expenses and make a pie graph to show your budget.

Then write a Lifestyle Essay. In this essay, discuss your job, justify your budget, and tell the reader what your life as a Lawyer is like. Finish the project by drawing a picture of you in your new car on the cover of your project folder.

Congratulations! You are a ROCK STAR!!!

You take home $7,500 a month. You pay $500 per month in rent and $500 for food. Now you decide. . . Look at your approved Car Buyer's Loan Payment worksheets. Look over your expenses and decide which car you will buy. Next, fill in your monthly expenses and make a pie graph to show your budget.

Then write a Lifestyle Essay. In this essay, discuss your job, justify your budget, and tell the reader what your life as a Rock Star is like. Finish the project by drawing a picture of you in your new car on the cover of your project folder.

Career Descriptions–2

Congratulations! You are a SECRETARY!!!

You take home $2,100 a month. You pay $700 per month in rent and $210 for food. Now you decide... Look at your approved Car Buyer's Loan Payment worksheets. Look over your expenses and decide which car you will buy. Next, fill in your monthly expenses and make a pie graph to show your budget.

Then write a Lifestyle Essay. In this essay, discuss your job, justify your budget, and tell the reader what your life as a Secretary is like. Finish the project by drawing a picture of you in your new car on the cover of your project folder.

Congratulations! You are a NEWSPAPER EDITOR!!!

You take home $2,700 a month. You pay $900 per month in rent and $270 for food. Now you decide... Look at your approved Car Buyer's Loan Payment worksheets. Look over your expenses and decide which car you will buy. Next, fill in your monthly expenses and make a pie graph to show your budget.

Then write a Lifestyle Essay. In this essay, discuss your job, justify your budget, and tell the reader what your life as a Newspaper Editor is like. Finish the project by drawing a picture of you in your new car on the cover of your project folder.

Congratulations! You are a MOVIE STAR!!!

You take home $7,000 a month. You pay $3,500 per month in rent and $700 for food. Now you decide... Look at your approved Car Buyer's Loan Payment worksheets. Look over your expenses and decide which car you will buy. Next, fill in your monthly expenses and make a pie graph to show your budget.

Then write a Lifestyle Essay. In this essay, discuss your job, justify your budget, and tell the reader what your life as a Movie Star is like. Finish the project by drawing a picture of you in your new car on the cover of your project folder.

Career Descriptions–3

Congratulations! You are a RESTAURANT MANAGER ! ! !

You take home $1,800 a month. You pay $450 per month in rent and $360 for food. Now you decide... Look at your approved Car Buyer's Loan Payment worksheets. Look over your expenses and decide which car you will buy. Next, fill in your monthly expenses and make a pie graph to show your budget.

Then write a Lifestyle Essay. In this essay, discuss your job, justify your budget, and tell the reader what your life as a Restaurant Manager is like. Finish the project by drawing a picture of you in your new car on the cover of your project folder.

Congratulations! You are an ENGINEER! ! !

You take home $3,500 a month. You pay $1,200 per month in rent and $450 for food. Now you decide... Look at your approved Car Buyer's Loan Payment worksheets. Look over your expenses and decide which car you will buy. Next, fill in your monthly expenses and make a pie graph to show your budget.

Then write a Lifestyle Essay. In this essay, discuss your job, justify your budget, and tell the reader what your life as an Engineer is like. Finish the project by drawing a picture of you in your new car on the cover of your project folder.

Congratulations! You are a BRAIN SURGEON! ! !

You take home $8,000 a month. You pay $2,000 per month in rent and $800 for food. Now you decide... Look at your approved Car Buyer's Loan Payment worksheets. Look over your expenses and decide which car you will buy. Next, fill in your monthly expenses and make a pie graph to show your budget.

Then write a Lifestyle Essay. In this essay, discuss your job, justify your budget, and tell the reader what your life as a Brain Surgeon is like. Finish the project by drawing a picture of you in your new car on the cover of your project folder.

Career Descriptions—4

Congratulations! You are a COMPUTER TECHNICIAN!!!

You take home $2,400 a month. You pay $800 per month in rent and $240 for food. Now you decide... Look at your approved Car Buyer's Loan Payment worksheets. Look over your expenses and decide which car you will buy. Next, fill in your monthly expenses and make a pie graph to show your budget.

Then write a Lifestyle Essay. In this essay, discuss your job, justify your budget, and tell the reader what your life as a Computer Technician is like. Finish the project by drawing a picture of you in your new car on the cover of your project folder.

Congratulations! You are a POSTAL CLERK!!!

You take home $2,600 a month. You pay $900 per month in rent and $250 for food. Now you decide... Look at your approved Car Buyer's Loan Payment worksheets. Look over your expenses and decide which car you will buy. Next, fill in your monthly expenses and make a pie graph to show your budget.

Then write a Lifestyle Essay. In this essay, discuss your job, justify your budget, and tell the reader what your life as a Postal Clerk is like. Finish the project by drawing a picture of you in your new car on the cover of your project folder.

Congratulations! You are a BANK LOAN OFFICER!!!

You take home $2,800 a month. You pay $750 per month in rent and $400 for food. Now you decide... Look at your approved Car Buyer's Loan Payment worksheets. Look over your expenses and decide which car you will buy. Next, fill in your monthly expenses and make a pie graph to show your budget.

Then write a Lifestyle Essay. In this essay, discuss your job, justify your budget, and tell the reader what your life as a Bank Loan Officer is like. Finish the project by drawing a picture of you in your new car on the cover of your project folder.

Mental Math Warm-Up

Find Percents • 1

To find 10 percent of a number, think of that number as a decimal.

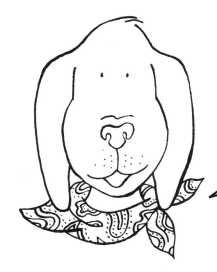

To find 10 percent of 20, make 20 into a decimal.
20 = 20.0
Then move the decimal point to the left one place.
10% of 20.0 = 2.00

Find 10 percent of the following numbers.

❶ 100   ❷ 30   ❸ 45

❹ 227   ❺ 555   ❻ 2,000

❼ 5.2   ❽ 0.3   ❾ 0.07

Find 15 percent of the following.

❶ 100   ❷ 1,000 ❸ 1,500

❹ 25   ❺ 49   ❻ 333

Mental Math Warm-Up   Find Percents • 2

You can find percent on any calculator.

It's simple to find percent with a calculator.
Try 25 percent of 350.
0.25 x 350 = ?
On your calculator:
    Type in 0.25 (for 25 percent).
    Press the x button.
    Type in 350.
    Press the = button.
You will discover:
    0.25 x 350 = 87.5

Study the pattern.

Pattern: Find 5 percent of 350 this way: 0.05 x 350 = ?
            Find 50 percent of 350 this way: 0.50 x 350 = ?
            Find 500 percent of 350 this way: 5.00 x 350 = ?

Write calculator equations for the following. Solve in your head or with a calculator.

❶ 7 percent of 280

❷ 70 percent of 280

❸ 700 percent of 280

❹ 25 percent of 78

❺ 25 percent of 1,000

❻ 2 percent of 100

❼ 120% of 100

❽ 200% of 350

❾ 2% of 3,254

❿ 33% of 300

Write your own instructions on how to find a percent on a calculator.

126   Using Fractions, Decimals and Percent

Mental Math Warm-Up   Compatible Decimals • 1

Compatible decimals add up to a whole number.

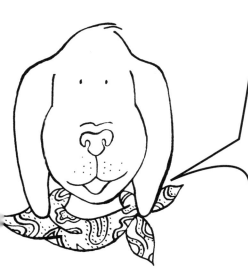

To add decimals, think fractions:
$0.4 + 0.6 = 1.0$
$\frac{4}{10}$ plus $\frac{6}{10}$ makes $\frac{10}{10}$.
Either way, you say 4 tenths plus 6 tenths make 10 tenths, or 1.

What about $0.30 + 0.70$?
That's 30 hundredths and 70 hundredths makes 100 hundredths, or 1.
$\frac{30}{100} + \frac{70}{100} = \frac{100}{100} = 1$

Find a decimal from the left that when added to a decimal from the right equals 1. Draw lines across to connect them. You will find five pairs and two leftovers.

0.05			0.6
	0.55	0.20	
0.30			0.39
	0.61	0.45	
			0.7
0.8		0.75	
	0.4		

Which decimals do not match?
Write a compatible decimal for each.

Match up five compatible decimal pairs for 10. That means that both decimals will add up to 10.

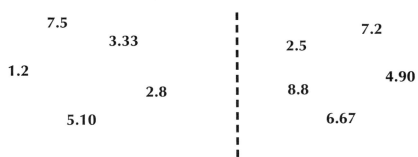

127

Mental Math Warm-Up   Compatible Decimals • 2

Compatible decimals add up to a whole number.

14.95 + 1.05 = 16
16 is a whole number.
4.35 + 4.65 = 9
9 is a whole number.
These ARE compatible decimals.

Find pairs of compatible decimals. Draw lines across to connect them.
You will find five pairs and two leftovers.

Which decimals do not match?
Write a compatible decimal for each.

For each of the following mixed decimals, write a compatible decimal that makes 10.

2.5   3.65   9.9

1.20   6.38   5.01

128   Using Fractions, Decimals and Percent

Mental Math Warm-Up

Compatible Decimals • 3

Compatible decimals for 10 add up to 10.

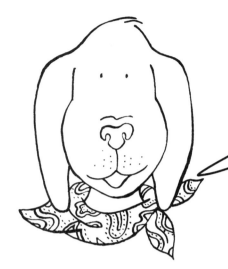

4.8 + 5.2 = 10
These are compatible for 10.

3.7 + 1.7 = 5.4
These ARE NOT compatible for 10, and they are not compatible decimals! (Remember: compatible decimals add up to a whole number.)

Find pairs of compatible decimals for 10. Draw lines across to connect them. You will find five pairs and two leftovers.

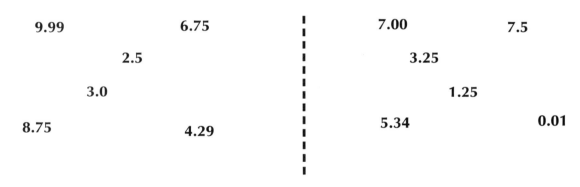

Which decimals do not match?
Write a compatible decimal for each.

For each of the numbers below, write a decimal that makes 10.

7.0   1.01   3.7

5.4   0.25   8.92

129

Mental Math Warm-Up

Friendly Fractions • 1

8 is what fraction of 16?

$$\frac{8}{16} = ?$$

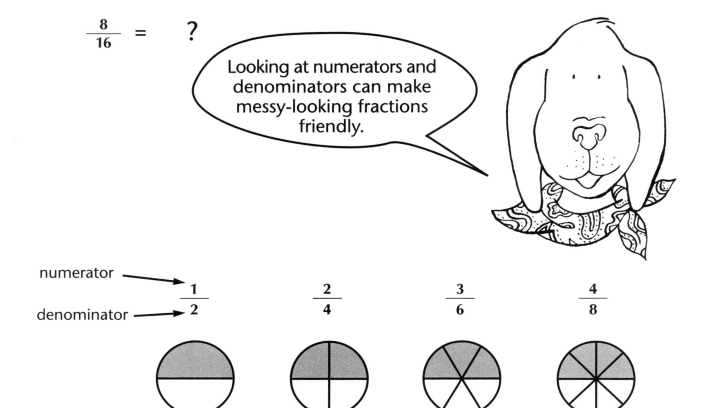

Looking at numerators and denominators can make messy-looking fractions friendly.

numerator → $\frac{1}{2}$ denominator →

$\frac{2}{4}$ $\frac{3}{6}$ $\frac{4}{8}$

Can you make these fractions friendlier?

$\frac{4}{16}$ $\frac{11}{88}$ $\frac{5}{20}$

$\frac{7}{21}$ $\frac{13}{39}$ $\frac{3}{32}$

MATH HOUND

Which fractions are equal? How can you tell?

$\frac{4}{12}$ $\frac{5}{20}$ $\frac{12}{36}$

$\frac{3}{9}$ $\frac{15}{60}$ $\frac{5}{15}$

Using Fractions, Decimals and Percent

Mental Math Warm-Up   Friendly Fractions • 2

Find a pattern in these fractions.

$$\frac{14}{21} \quad \frac{2}{3}$$

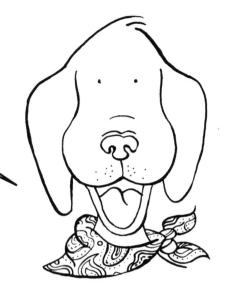

Here's a hint. What number goes into both the numerator and denominator?

$$\frac{14}{21} \div \frac{7}{7} = \frac{2}{3}$$

What fractions do these circles show?

Find the friendly fractions.

❶ $\frac{23}{46}$ ❷ $\frac{14}{28}$ ❸ $\frac{9}{27}$

❹ $\frac{6}{18}$ ❺ $\frac{16}{32}$ ❻ $\frac{18}{36}$

❼ $\frac{15}{20}$ ❽ $\frac{1}{12}$ ❾ $\frac{10}{15}$

Which two fractions when added together will equal more than 1? How do you know?

$$\frac{7}{15} \qquad \frac{5}{9} \qquad \frac{3}{7}$$
$$\frac{6}{11} \qquad \frac{4}{10}$$

131

Mental Math Warm-Up

Estimating Fractions

Estimate fractions by finding close-by friendly fractions.

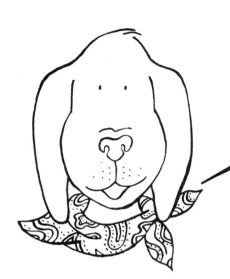

We have 29 in our class. Are 15 students about half the class?
29 is close to 30.
$\frac{15}{30}$ is half.
So $\frac{15}{29}$ is about half.

What are these fractions almost (nearly) worth? Estimate by finding close-by friendly fractions.

❶ $\frac{9}{20}$ ❷ $\frac{7}{12}$ ❸ $\frac{2}{15}$

❹ $\frac{39}{50}$ ❺ $\frac{11}{24}$ ❻ $\frac{2}{9}$

❼ $\frac{12}{49}$ ❽ $\frac{9}{29}$ ❾ $\frac{13}{25}$

❿ $\frac{4}{15}$

Find other fractions equal to fractions ❶ to ❷.

Using Fractions, Decimals and Percent

Bibliography

BOOKS FOR THE STUDENT

Cribb, Joe. **Money**. New York: Alfred A. Knopf, 1990. This eyewitness book has a wealth of pictures and facts about coins and bills from around the world. With index and a guide to worldwide currency.

James, Elizabeth, and Carol Barkin. **How to Grow a Hundred Dollars.** New York: Lothrop, Lee & Shepard, 1979. A fiction book about a girl who starts a business and learns about costs, inflation, profit and loss, interest and loans, and attracting new investors. Includes an index.

Maestro, Betsy. **The Story of Money.** New York: Clarion Books, 1993. A history of money, from barter systems in ancient times to the use of coins and paper money, as well as modern cashless transactions.

Meltzer, Milton. **Gold!** New York: HarperCollins, 1993. Discusses the value of gold and how it has been sought after and used in countries around the world throughout history. Includes index and bibliography.

Merrill, Jean. The **Toothpaste Millionaire.** Boston: Houghton Mifflin, 1972. A fiction story about a 12-year-old boy who creates a cheaper tube of toothpaste. His company prospers and he eventually issues stock.

Pierce, Catherine Doris. **To Market, To Market!** Palo Alto, CA: Toyon Press, 1993. Describes the history and workings of the New York Stock Exchange through the story of a start-up company that needs funds. Contains a helpful glossary of essential terms. Available from Toyon Press, 920 Barbara Dr., Palo Alto, CA 94303.

Pinczes, Elinor. **One Hundred Hungry Ants.,** New York: Houghton Mifflin, 1993. One hundred hungry ants head toward a picnic to get yummies for their tummies, but stops to change their line formation, showing different divisions of 100, causing them to lose both time and food in the end.

Schwartz, David M. **How Much Is a Million?** New York: Scholastic Inc., 1985. Uses concepts in nature and everyday life to help readers conceptualize millions, billions, and trillions. A picture book that might help for review.

Schwartz, David M. **If You Made a Million.** New York: Lothrop, Lee & Shepard, 1989. Describes the various forms that money can take, including coins, paper money, and personal checks, and how it can be used to make purchases, pay off loans, or build interest in the bank. A picture book interesting enough for older students.

BOOKS FOR THE TEACHER

Gillespie, Janet and Patsy Kanter. **Every Day Counts™ Kit**. Wilmington, MA: Great Source Education Group, 1994. Uses an interactive bulletin board to develop understanding of key math concepts and skills.

Index

Absolute value, 50-54
Addition
 of decimals, 43, 50-54
 of money, 76-89
Advertisements
 understanding, 76-78
 writing, 86-89
Assessment
 about, 17
 Assessment 1: Write About Decimals, 20-24
 Assessment 2: Estimate and Order Decimals, 50-54
 Assessment 3: Mini-Portfolio, 106-110
  evaluation checklists, 112-113
  Self-Evaluation of Car Buyer's Project, 90-96

Bar graph, 76-77
Benchmark, 50-54
Bibliography, 133

Calculator, 34-35, 38-41, 50-54, 66-72, 76-84, 98-99
Chart, 29, 34-35, 99
Circle graph, 72, 84-85
Classroom organization See Cooperative learning and Teaching Tips.
Communication
 discussing, 29, 57, 63, 65, 85, 99, 101-104,
 presenting and sharing 35, 39, 43, 65, 67, 87, 101
 talking and writing about math, 10
 writing, 29, 32-33, 47, 49, 51, 80-83
Comparing
 bar and circle graphs, 84-85
 and ordering decimals, 48-54
 and ordering large numbers, 76-79
 and ordering mixed decimals, 42-45
 scales in graphs, 98-99
Consumer issues
 calculating sales tax, 72
 calculating a tip, 72
 creating a business, 32-33
 developing a personal budget, 76-83
 economic systems, 30-31
 evaluating an investment, 102-104
 interest, 76-83
 Law of Supply and Demand, 29-30, 102-104
 reading data from a stock table, 35
 understanding a newspaper ad, 76-77
 writing a newspaper ad, 86-89

Cooperative learning, 34-36, 50-54, 62-71, 86-89
Curriculum integration, 13-14. See *also* Consumer issues, Literature, and Social studies.

Data analysis
  analyzing data from graph, 84-85, 98-104
  collecting data from story, 56-61
  See *also* Chart, Graphing, and Scale.
Decimals
  comparing and ordering decimals, 42-45, 48-49
  dividing, 35, 70-82, 102-104
  mixed, 42-47
  modeling, 48-49, 62-65
  multiplying, 70-72, 76-89
  place value in, 38-41, 46-47
  reading, 42-45
  relating to fractions, 64-69
  representing percent as, 62-63
  rounding, 42-45
  subtracting, 43, 48-54
  zero in, 46-47
Degrees of a circle, 85
Division
  of money, 35, 72, 102-104
  by powers of ten, 38-41, 64-71
  using whole numbers and decimals, 70-71

Economics See Consumer issues.
Equations, 71-72, 80-83, 86-89
Estimation, 38-41, 50-54
Exponential notation, 64-72
Extensions/Homework, 29, 43, 63, 72, 77, 85, 87, 99, 101, 103

Family involvement, 16
Fractions
  of a dollar, 41, 62-63, 98-101
  relating to decimals, 64-69
  representing percent as, 62-63

Games, 46-54, 70-71
Graphing
  bar graph, 84-85
  circle graph, 72, 84-85
  line graph, 98-99
  time line, 56-61 See *also* Chart, Data analysis, and Scale.
Homework, See Extensions/Homework.

Interest, 76-83

Line graph, 98-101
Literature
  If You Made a Million by David M. Schwartz, 70-71
  One Hundred Hungry Ants by Elinor J. Pinczes, 64-69
  The Story of Money by Betsy Maestro, 56-61
  The Toothpaste Millionaire by Jean Merrill, 98-99,103

Manipulatives
  base-ten blocks, 38-41
  compass, 85
Measurement See Scale and Modeling.
Mental math, 35, 62-63, 77, 81, 85, 87, 91, 99, 101
Modeling
  geometric, 38-41, 62-69
Money
  calculating with, 34, 72, 76-89, 98-104
  fractions of a dollar, 41, 62-65
  percents of money, 62-63, 72, 86-89
  rounding to the nearest penny, 76-79 See *also* Consumer issues.
Multiplication
  of money, 72, 76-79
  by powers of ten, 38-41
  using whole numbers and decimals, 70-71

Number
  connecting visual and symbolic representations for, 38-41, 62-69
  ordering, 38-45, 48-54
  ordering on a number line, 41-45, 51
  word names, 38-49, 64-65
Number line, 41-45, 51
Number sentences See Equations.

Pattern
  observing, 38-41, 98-99
Percent
  concepts, 62-63
  of money, 62-63, 76-79, 86-89
  representing as fractions and decimals, 62-63
Place value, 38-41, 46-47, 70-71
Projects
  Car Buyer's Project, 74-86
  The Stock Market Project, 26-36, 98-104

Reasoning, 38-54, 56-72, 76-85, 87, 98-104
Rounding, 42-45, 51, 76-79

Scale
  choosing for a bar graph, 84-85
  choosing for a line graph, 98-101
  choosing for a time line, 56-61
Social studies
  history of coin composition, 57
  history of human culture, 56-61
  history of stock markets, 31
Subtraction
  of decimals, 43, 48-54
  of money, 76-89

Teacher Reproducible Pages, 112-132
Teaching Tips
  about line graphs, 99
  about student self-assessment, 91
  background information, 72
  building skills, 47
  classroom management, 29
  making connections, 63
  managing the activity, 87
  meeting individual needs, 36, 43, 49
  modeling correct responses, 71
  questioning strategies, 65, 67
  reaching all learners, 35, 45, 51
  sharing ideas, 68
  using critical thinking: observation skills, 58
  using logical reasoning, 35
Time line, 56, 61, 72

Visual thinking, 38-41, 62-69
Vocabulary
  glossary of stock terms, 31

Whole class activities, 28-33, 38-41, 46-54, 56-69, 76-89, 98-99
Write About Math, 29, 47-49, 67, 103
Writing
  in assessment, 20-24, 50-54, 106-110
  book review for younger readers, 67
  brochure, 101
  a business letter, 29
  a car ad, 87
  equations, 63
  Lifestyle Essay, 81

Zero, 46-47

STUDENT ACTIVITY PAGES

SECTION 9

WRITE ABOUT DECIMALS	S-1
STOCK TABLE SLEUTHS	S-2
STOCK RECORDING SHEET	S-3
PLACE VALUE PATTERNS	S-4
HOW CLOSE CAN YOU GET?	S-5
LARGEST AND SMALLEST	S-6
DATA SHEET FROM *THE STORY OF MONEY*	S-7
PLAN YOUR TIME LINE	S-8
PICTURE PARTS OF A DOLLAR	S-9
FIND PERCENTS	S-10
PICTURE DECIMALS WITH CENTIMETER SQUARES	S-11
PARTS OF DECIMALS	S-12
MORE PARTS OF DECIMALS	S-13
CHALLENGE: FIND THE WHOLE FROM THE PART	S-14
THE ANTS' PICNIC	S-15
TINIER AND TINIER	S-16
HOW TO PLAY GET OFF THE FIELD!	S-17
RECORDING SHEET FOR GET OFF THE FIELD!	S-18
CAR BUYER'S PROJECT • PHASE I	S-19

(continued on next page)

Car Buyer's Loan Worksheet	S-20
Monthly Budget Practice Sheet	S-21
My Monthly Budget	S-22
Car Buyer's Project • Phase II • Organize Your Work	S-23
Make a Pie Graph from a bar Graph	S-24
Car Buyer's Project • Phase III	S-25
Resale Worksheet	S-26
Car Buyer's Project • Self-evaluation	S-27
Car Buyer's Project • Grading Your Own Work	S-28
Toothpaste Shareholder's Math-1	S-29
Toothpaste Shareholder's Math-2	S-30
Did Your Stock Grow in Value?	S-31
Mini-portfolio	S-32

Name _____   Date _____

Write About Decimals

1. Think about what you already know about decimals. List your ideas on a separate sheet of paper. Then underline two ideas that you think are the most important.

   Explain why these ideas are important for understanding decimals.

2. How are decimals like money? How are they different from money?

3. How are decimals like fractions? How are they different from fractions? Give specific examples. Use pictures if you want.

Stock Table Sleuths

Name ____________

NASDAQ Listings

Quotations as of 4 p.m. Eastern Time
Wednesday, August 16, 1995

52 Weeks Hi	52 Weeks Lo	Stock	Sym	Div	Yld %	PE	Vol 100s	Hi	Lo	Close	Net Chg
		-A-A-A-									
13 55/64	6 3/4	AAON Inc	AAON	p	...	10	45	7 3/4	7 1/2	7 1/2	...
12 7/8	9	ABC Bcp	ABCB	.30	2.4	11	18	12 3/4	12 1/2	12 3/4	+ 1/4
27 5/8	19	ABC RailPdt	ABCR		...	23	264	24 3/4	24 1/8	24 1/8	− 3/4
23 1/2	8 21/32	ABR InfoSvc	ABRX		...	55	248	20 1/4	19 1/4	20 1/4	+ 3/4
14 1/2	10 1/4	♣ABS Ind	ABSI	.20	2.0	11	12	10 1/4	10 1/4	10 1/4	...
19 3/4	11 7/8	ABT BldgPdt	ABTC		...	11	237	19 1/4	19	19 1/4	+ 1/4
19 3/4	**13**	**ACC**	**ACCC**	**.12**	**.7**	**dd**	**592**	**17 1/2**	**16 1/2**	**17 1/4**	**+ 7/8**
19	5 1/2	ACS Ent	ACSE		...	dd	219	18 1/2	17 3/4	18 1/4	+ 3/8
13 1/2	3 1/4	Activision	ATVI		...	dd	709	12	11	11 3/4	...
26 3/4	12 5/8	Acxiom	ACXM		...	31	1690	25	24 1/4	24 1/4	− 1/4
13 3/4	6 1/4	AdacLabs	ADAC	.48	3.7	15	59	13 1/4	12 7/8	13	− 1/16
6 5/8	4 3/8	Adage	ADGE		...	dd	18	6	5 3/4	6	+ 1/8
47 1/4	17 1/4	Adaptec	ADPT		...	23	7622	47 1/8	46 1/4	47	+ 3/4
9 1/8	6 1/16	AdcoTch	ADCO	.03e	.3	...	23	9	8 5/8	8 63/64	− 1/64
15 1/4	8	AddintnRes	ADDR		...	dd	337	13 7/8	13 1/2	13 7/8	+ 5/16
15 1/2	7 1/2	AdelphiaComm	ADLAC		...	dd	275	10 1/2	10 1/8	10 3/8	...
29 1/4	13 1/2	ADFlexSol	AFLX		...	21	666	27 1/2	26 3/4	26 7/8	− 1/4
27	19 3/8	Adia adr	ADIAY		...	...	22	23 1/4	23 1/4	23 1/4	+ 3/4
66 1/2	**27 1/4**	**♣AdobeSys**	**ADBE**	**.20**	**.3**	**99**	**16564**	**63 1/2**	**59 3/4**	**63 1/4**	**+ 4**
22 1/4	9 1/4	AdvCircuit	ADVC		...	17	7400	22 3/16	21 1/8	22	− 1/8
31 3/4	17 1/4	♣AdvRoss	AROS		...	16	11	31 1/2	31	31 1/2	+ 11/16
7 5/8	3 5/8	AdvLogicRsrch	AALR		...	31	381	6 3/4	6 3/8	6 3/4	+ 3/16
7 3/8	**5 1/4**	**AdvMktg**	**ADMS**		**...**	**11**	**2**	**7**	**7**	**7**	**− 3/8**
4 1/4	**2 1/8**	**AdvNMRSys**	**ANMR**		**...**	**...**	**1511**	**2 7/8**	**2 11/16**	**2 7/8**	**+ 3/16**
7 1/8	4	♣AdvPolymer	APOS		...	dd	158	6 3/8	6 1/8	6 3/8	...
42 3/8	2 3/8	AdvSemi	ASMIF		...	...	1336	40 3/4	39 1/2	40	+ 1/2
19 1/2	13	AdvTchLab	ATLI		...	dd	244	17 1/2	17 1/4	17 1/4	...

1. Find Adobe Systems on NASDAQ. What is its closing price? HINT: Look under Close.____________

2. Find IBM on the NYSE. What is its closing price?

____

HINTS: It is the abbreviation for International Business Machines. Look under Last.

NYSE Listings

52 Week High	52 Week Low	Stock	Div	PE	Sales 100s	Last	Net Chg
		—I—					
50 3/4	29 1/8	IBP	.20	9	974	49	
5	2 3/8	ICF Int			117	4 1/4	+ 3/8
23 1/8	12 1/4	ICN Ph n	.28b	12	938	20 3/8	
27 7/8	20 3/8	IES	2.10	12	377	24 1/8	+ 3/8
63 1/4	36 1/4	IMC Glob	.30e	15	1347	59 3/4	− 3/8
21 1/4	12 1/2	IMCO	.17e	22	1125	20 3/4	
26 1/2	19 3/4	IPTimb	2.88a	4	254	22 1/4	
27 5/8	14 7/8	IRSA n			38	24 1/2	− 3/8
10 1/2	8 3/4	IRT	.90f	17	357	9 7/8	
16	12 5/8	ISS Int	.20e		1	13 1/8	− 1/8
121 7/8	77	ITT Cp	1.98	21	3475	116 3/4	+ 1/4
153 1/2	101 1/8	ITT pfNcld	2.25		21	147 1/4	
19 1/4	9 1/2	ITT Ed n		28	87	18 7/8	+ 1/8
26 3/4	22	IdahoP	1.86	14	683	25 7/8	+ 1/4
21 3/8	8 3/8	Ideon	.20		3381	9 3/4	
44 1/4	25 3/4	Idex s	.56	20	104	41 1/4	− 3/8
40 7/8	28 5/8	IlliCtr	1.00	15	2195	40 1/8	− 1/8
27	23 7/8	IllPC pfM	2.36		37	26 3/4	
27	21 1/2	IlPow pfA	2.04		z200	27	+1
61 3/4	39 5/8	ITW	.68f	20	774	58 5/8	
26	18 1/8	Illinova	1.00	12	1728	25	+ 1/4
12 1/2	6 1/8	ImoInd		11	188	9	
53 1/2	43 1/2	ICI	2.18e	18	1759	49	− 1/4
35 5/8	23 1/2	INCO	.40	20	8903	36 1/8	+1 1/4
14	8 3/4	IndiaFd	.13e		916	10 3/8	− 1/4
25 1/8	17	IndiaG	.92e		68	18 1/8	− 1/8
21 7/8	17 1/2	IndiEngy	1.10f	13	133	18 7/8	− 1/8
15 1/2	9 3/8	Indones			65	11 3/4	
40 3/4	30 1/8	IndoSat n	.38p		4181	34	−1 1/2
16 3/8	10 7/8	Indresc		13	3984	16 3/4	+ 1/2
38 1/4	29 7/8	IndNatuz	.09e	22	798	35 1/4	− 1/4
37 5/8	18 3/8	InmnBr s		56	602	36 3/8	+ 5/8
42 1/8	28 3/8	IngerRd	.74	18	2470	40 5/8	+ 3/8
42	23 1/2	InldStl	.20	9	1267	28 1/8	+ 3/8
41 3/4	16 23/32	InputOut		29	1218	38 1/2	−1
9	6 7/8	Insteel	.24	8	125	7 3/4	+ 1/4
12	9 3/8	InsMuni	.77		471	11 1/8	
20 3/8	11 3/4	Integon	.36	13	678	16	− 3/8
53 61/64	43 5/8	Integn pf	3.88		1	52	− 1/4
54 7/8	36 7/8	IntegFn	2.00	11	189	51 1/8	+ 1/8
42 1/2	25 1/4	IntgHS	.02e	12	1284	28 5/8	+ 1/4
7 1/4	3	Intelcal			57	5 1/8	− 1/8
31 3/4	21 3/4	IFG	.64	11	58	31 3/8	+ 1/8
12 5/8	9 1/8	IntrCal	.75		243	11 3/4	+ 1/4
11 3/8	8 1/2	IntCAQI	.72		175	10 3/8	+ 1/8
18 1/4	15 1/8	ItcpSe	1.44		39	16 1/4	
15 1/2	11 5/8	IntcapIn	1.02		52	14 3/8	− 1/8
9	5 1/2	Interco s		11	96	7 1/2	− 1/8
3 1/4	1 1/2	Intrlke			416	2 1/2	− 1/8
21 5/8	7 1/8	IntlCer n			33	8 1/8	+ 1/8
36 3/4	26 3/8	IntAlu	1.00	11	36	34 1/8	+ 1/8
112 1/8	63 3/4	IBM	1.00	13	29468	112 3/8	+ 3/8

Below are the August 16 facts for Adobe Systems. On a separate sheet of paper, answer these questions, showing all equations. Convert fractions to dollars and cents. ($1\frac{1}{4}$ is $1.25.)

1. How much did a share of Adobe stock cost at closing on August 16? The day before?
2. What was the 52-week high price for a share of Adobe stock? 52-week low price?
3. If you owned 100 shares of Adobe stock, how much would you get in yearly dividends?

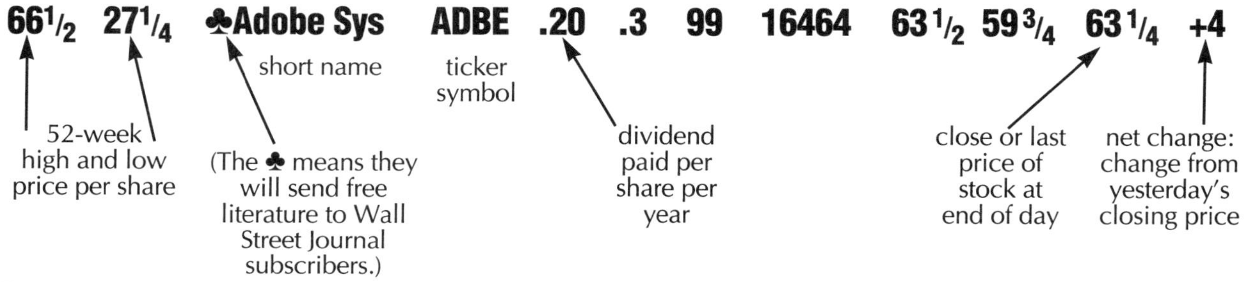

Stock Recording Sheet

Name _____

Name of stock: _____

Ticker symbol and Wall Street Journal Abbreviation:

Where is the stock listed? Circle one:

    NYSE   NASDAQ   Amex

Name of newspaper where the stock is reported: _____

Date of Newspaper	Close/Last Price*	Date of Newspaper	Close/Last Price*

*You may record your price as a fraction. We will convert to dollars at the end of the project.

Place Value Patterns

Name _____

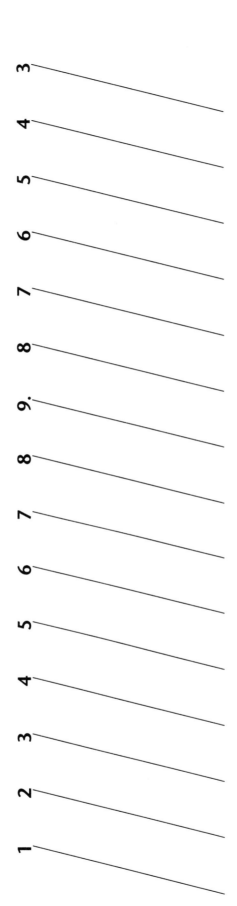

1. Identify the decimal point in the number above.

2. Write the place value names for each whole number part of this mixed decimal.

3. Predict the name for each decimal place.

4. Use your math journal. Describe one or more patterns you see in the place value names for whole numbers and decimals.

How Close Can You Get?

Name _____

1. Cut out the squares below.
   Arrange the digits to make a number that rounds to 50.
   Record your number_____.
   Explain why your number rounds to 50.

2. Now rearrange the digits to make at least two other numbers that round to 50. Record each number.

3. Choose one of the numbers you have made.
   Write it in words, using whole numbers and decimal place values.

4. Compare the decimals you have made.
   Which one is **closest to 50?** Explain how you know.

✂ -

| . | 0 | 4 | 3 | 5 | 7 | 9 |

S-5

Largest and Smallest

Name _____

1. What is the SMALLEST number that uses all of the digits and rounds to 50?

   Explain how you know that this is the smallest number.

   Use a number line to prove your answer.

   ———————————————50———————————————

2. What is the **LARGEST** number that uses all the digits and rounds to 50?

   Explain how you know that this is the largest number.

   Use a number line to prove your answer.

   ———————————————50———————————————

CHALLENGE: HOW LOW CAN YOU GO?

   Look through newspapers and magazines for decimals and fractions.

   Copy or cut out examples of the smallest numbers you can find.

Data Sheet from *The Story of Money*

Name _____

Read ***The Story of Money.*** Find information in the book that will help you make a time line. Write it in the boxes below.

Who?	Dates	Kind of economy	What did they use for money?
Early peoples (before Catal Huyuk)	2,500,000 B.C.	hunters/gatherers	They didn't need any.
People of Catal Huyuk			
Sumerian traders			
Lydian traders			
Chinese empire at the time of Marco Polo			
Spanish Empire			
Colonial America			
The early United States			
Money today			

Plan Your Time Line

Name _____

EXAMINE A SAMPLE TIME LINE	CHECK YOUR DATA FROM *THE STORY OF MONEY*
1. What data does the sample time line show?	1. What data will your time line show? Give your time line a title.
2. What period of time does the sample time line cover?	2. What period of time does your data cover? *About how many years are there between the period of early man and the Sumerians?* *About how many years are there between the Sumerians and the Lydians?* *About how many years are there between the Lydian culture and Marco Polo's travels to China?*
3. What intervals does the sample use?	3. What intervals will you make? Why? Think about the size of your paper. How will you fit in the data?
4. What scale does the sample use?	4. What scale will you use to fit your time line onto the paper? How did you figure it out?

Picture Parts of a Dollar

Name _____

What do you notice about the dollar bill in the picture?

How much would one rectangle be worth?

Color 1/4 of the dollar green.
Color 1/2 of the dollar red.
Color 1/5 of the dollar yellow.
Color 1/20 of the dollar brown.

Then fill in the values on the chart.

	Fraction of a dollar	Decimal (money notation)	Percent
The green part of the dollar is worth			
The red part of the dollar is worth			
The yellow part of the dollar is worth			
The brown part of the dollar is worth			

Find Percents

Name _____

"Per cent" means parts of a hundred. We show percent with %.

If you have one cent, you have $\frac{1}{100}$ or 1% of a dollar.

If you have 33 cents, you have $\frac{33}{100}$ or 33% of a dollar.

If the bone was $2.00, how much will it cost on sale? It helps to think of fractions— 50% is $\frac{50}{100}$, or half!

☞ When you find percents, think of fractions.

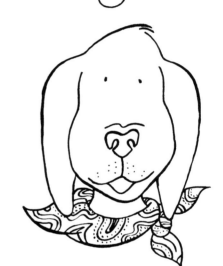

SOLVE.

1. Find 10% of $1.00   (What is $\frac{1}{10}$ of a dollar?)

2. Find 10% of $4.00.   (What is $\frac{1}{10}$ of 4 dollars?)

3. Find 10% of $40.00. (What is $\frac{1}{10}$ of 40 dollars?)

4. Find 10% of $400.00. (What is $\frac{1}{10}$ of 400 dollars?)

Write About Math:

Look for a pattern in the placement of the decimal point in questions 1-4. In your math journal, write a rule for finding 10% of any amount.

Use the 10% rule for these.

5. 10% of $14.95   6. 10% of $199.99   7. 10% of $73,000.00

Use what you know of the 10% rule to find 15% of these.

8. 15% of $10.00   9. 15% of $50.00   10. 15% of $25.00

Picture Decimals with Centimeter Squares

Name _____

WHAT YOU NEED:

- *graph paper*
- *colored pencils or markers*
- *calculator (optional)*

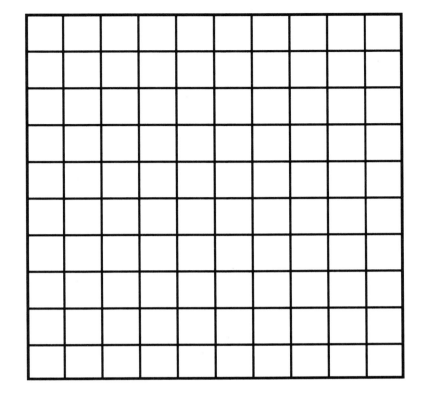

The large square is worth one.

1. How much is one small square worth? Explain how you figured out your answer.

2. How much are ten small squares worth?

3. How much are 100 small squares worth?

4. Use colored markers to show the following decimals on the grid. Use a different color for each decimal.

   a. 0.3 b. 0.03 c. 0.035

Label each colored area three ways:

   using decimal notation

   using fraction notation

   using words

Parts of Decimals

Name _____

Decimals are great when you are figuring out tenths and hundredths of things.
But how do you find a half of a tenth or a half of a hundredth?

WHAT YOU NEED:

- *graph paper*
- *colored pencils or markers*
- *calculator (optional)*

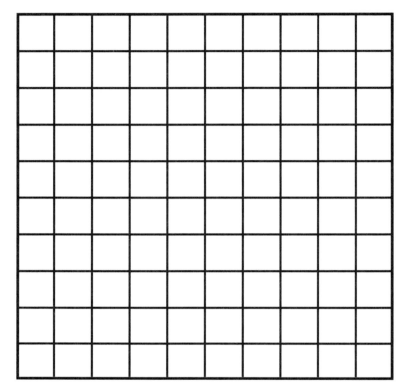

1. Use the picture to show half of 50 hundredths.

2. Then write a decimal for your picture. _____

3. Explain how you figured out the decimal that is half of 0.50.

4. Also write your decimal as a fraction. _____

5. Now try these. Draw a picture for each on graph paper.

    a. half of 36 hundredths

    b. one third of 75 hundredths

    c. one fourth of 80 hundredths

    d. one sixth of 24 hundredths

More Parts of Decimals

Name _____

1. Use pictures to show the given parts of a whole.

2. Write a decimal and a fraction for each picture you create.

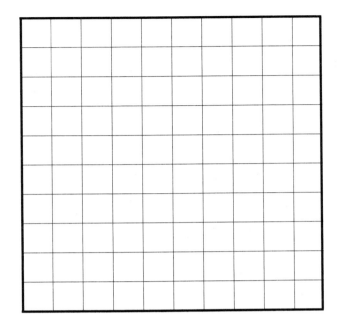

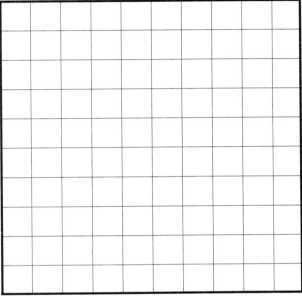

b) one fourth of 10 hundredths

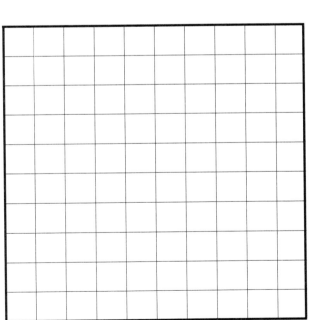

c) two thirds of 60 hundredths

S-13

Challenge: Find the Whole from the Part

Name _____

HERE'S THE CHALLENGE:

The shaded part shows 0.125 of a whole.
What does one unit look like? Draw it.
Explain how you figured out your answer.

S-14

The Ants' Picnic

Name _____

*One thousand ants are coming to the picnic.
They will share one brownie fairly.*

"Yum! I see lots of pieces. I wonder if there are enough for everyone."

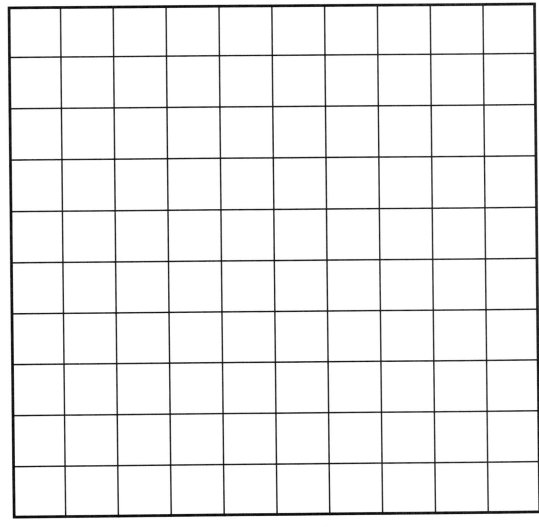

"This is a pretty big brownie!"

1. Decide how to make a fair share for one ant—that is, exactly one thousandth of a brownie. Show what a fair share would look like. Use a calculator if you need help.

2. Prove that your drawing shows a fair share for one of 1,000 ants. Write how you figured it out in your math journal.

Tinier and Tinier

Name _____

What you need:

- math journal
- centimeter graph paper
- colored pencils or markers

Solve:

1. What fraction of the brownie is one teeny tiny square? Explain how you figured out your answer in your journal.
2. How much are ten teeny tiny squares?
3. How much are 100 teeny tiny squares?
4. Use a different color to show each of the following decimals:

   a. 0.345   b. 0.0345   c. 3.45

"This is one big brownie!"

How to Play Get Off the Field!   Name _____

> **WHAT YOU NEED:**
> - recording sheet, S-18
> - game board (page 118) with game pieces cut out
> - scratch paper
> - calculators (optional)

OBJECT OF THE GAME

Try to be the first to get off the field. This can be done by accumulating 5 points or by arriving at Millions or Millionths with an exact draw of a card.

HOW TO GET POINTS

a correct equation to get to Millions   =   1 point
a correct equation to get to Millionths   =   2 points

SET UP THE GAME

1. Each player draws an oval Player Card to determine the order of play.
2. Players put their Player Cards in the ones place on the game board.
3. Shuffle the square cards.

HOW TO PLAY

1. Player One draws a square card and moves to the destination on the card. If the destination is off the board, the player cannot move.

2. Player One says, "I want to get off the field by going to Millions (or Millionths)." Then Player One writes an equation (not using a calculator) that would get him to Millions or Millionths after making the move; the answer will have to be 1,000,000 or 1/1,000,000. Other players check his equation with their calculators. If Player One was correct, he gets a point or points.

3. Then Player Two takes a turn. She draws a card and moves. She announces her plan to get off the field and writes her equation. The other players check her math with their calculators. She gets a point or points if her math was correct.

4. Each player takes a turn, drawing, moving, and writing equations.

5. After everyone has had two turns, a winner can be declared. There are two ways to win: accumulate 5 points or land exactly on Millions or Millionths.

Recording Sheet for Get Off the Field!

Name _____

My card took me to	I want to reach	This equation will get me there	Points
Sample thousands	millions	1,000 x 1,000 = 1,000,000	1

1. Play the game with a partner or group.
2. In your math journal, explain how you move your marker to a bigger number. Do you multiply or divide?
3. Then write about how you move your marker to a smaller number.

Car Buyer's Project • Phase I

What information is in a newspaper ad?

1. Pretend you are talking with a friend over the telephone about buying a car.

2. Describe one of the cars advertised below.

3. Then practice filling out a sample Car Buyer's Loan Worksheet (page S-20) using the information in this ad or one your teacher displays.

> PORSCHE '83 944 AT, loaded, like nu. Red. 114K mi. sunrf. Excel. running cond. $5900.
>
> FORD '94 Mustang, 1 owner, 20K mi., immac., AT, PS, AC, PW, ABS, cruise, cass., spoiler. $11.9 or BO.

NOW you are ready to look for used cars to buy.

WHAT YOU NEED:

- *Car Buyer's Loan Worksheets (3 copies)*
- *newspaper ads or car brochures*
- *daily interest rate (posted)*
- *calculator (optional)*

You can use classified ads from the newspaper or other brochures that advertise new cars. You don't know yet what kind of car you can afford but you can dream both small and big.

Choose three possible cars to buy. One car must cost less than $10,000. One car must cost between $10,000 and $20,000. One car must cost more than $20,000.

Car Buyer's Loan Worksheet

Name _____

Attach ad if possible.

Make: _____

Model: _____

Year: _____

Mileage: _____

Options: _____

Retail price: _____

Financing this car

Today's date: _____

Retail price: _____

Down payment (10%): _____

Amount to finance: _____

Today's interest rate _____

times amount to finance: _____

Total financed amount: _____

Term of loan (months): _____

Total monthly payment: _____

Monthly Budget Practice Sheet

Name _____

Your monthly income is: _____

Your monthly budget must include:

Housing _____

Food _____

Car Payment _____

Car Insurance _____
    (Assume 10% of retail
    price per year. Sports cars,
    12%.)

Entertainment _____

Clothing _____

Savings _____

Other _____

NOTE: Your budget must add up exactly to your monthly income.

My Monthly Budget

Name _____

```
┌─ ─ ─ ─ ─ ─ ─ ─ ─ ─ ─ ─ ─ ─ ─ ─ ─ ─ ─ ─ ─ ─ ─ ─ ─ ─ ─ ─ ─ ─ ─ ─ ┐
│                                                                │
│                                                                │
│              paste your career data sheet here                 │
│                                                                │
│                                                                │
└─ ─ ─ ─ ─ ─ ─ ─ ─ ─ ─ ─ ─ ─ ─ ─ ─ ─ ─ ─ ─ ─ ─ ─ ─ ─ ─ ─ ─ ─ ─ ─ ┘
```

My monthly income is: _____

My monthly budget must include:

Housing _____

Food _____

Car Payment _____

Car Insurance _____
    (Assume 10% of retail price per
    year. Sports cars, 12%.)

Entertainment _____

Clothing _____

Savings _____

Other _____

NOTE: Your budget must add up to exactly your monthly income. Look at your expenses. Then study your approved Car Buyer's Loan Worksheets and decide which car you can afford to buy.

Car Buyer's Project • Phase II
• Organize Your Work

Name _____

You have chosen a career at random. You know how much you earn every month and how much you need for food, housing, and other expenses. You have chosen the right car for your budget.

1. Write a Lifestyle Essay. In your essay, tell the reader what career you chose and what your life is like. Explain how you decided on your budget and why you chose the car you did.

2. Make a Project Folder. Include the following in your folder:
   - Car Payment Plan for the car you decide to buy
   - your other approved Car Buyer's Loan Worksheets
   - your Lifestyle Essay
   - a cover illustration that shows you in your new car

Make a Pie Graph from a Bar Graph

WHAT YOU NEED:

- graph paper
- your monthly budget figures
- colored markers or crayons
- tape
- scissors
- ruler
- a clean sheet of paper
- calculator

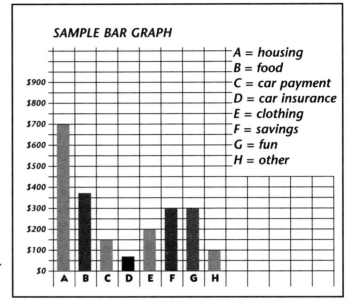

1. Make a bar graph of your monthly expenses.

   Color each category in a different color.

2. Write a fraction for each category.

   Use a calculator to convert each fraction into a decimal and a percent.

   To convert a fraction to a decimal, divide the numerator by the denominator.
   700 ÷ 2,200 = .3181818
   Round to the nearest hundredth.
   $32/100$ is the same as 32 out of 100, or 32%.

   $$\frac{700}{2,200} = 0.32$$

3. Cut out the bars from your graph and tape the pieces together into one long bar.

   Bring the ends together to make a circle.

   Tape your circle onto a sheet of clean paper.

   Use a ruler to make a straight a line for each section to the center of the circle. Color each section to match the bar graph.

Car Buyer's Project • Phase III

Name _____

It is now . . . Three Years Later!

You got a promotion and a raise. You decide it is time to buy a more presentable car. You decide to sell your car the same way you bought it, through a classified ad. Now you need to decide how much to ask for your used car.

1. Answer these questions:

    A. How old is your car now? _____

    B. How many miles are on the car now? (The average driver puts 12,000 miles per year on his or her car.) _____

    C. What is the condition of your car? (Have you had any accidents? Did you regularly change the oil and rotate the tires? Are the brakes in good working order?)

    D. What price did you pay for the car when you bought it? _____

    E. Is there anything extra special that you added to your car that would make it a better buy? _____

2. Now use the Resale Worksheet on page S-26 to calculate a fair asking price. Show how you calculated each line item.

3. Write a want ad to place your car for sale in a local newspaper. Include only necessary information. Newspapers charge by the word and by the space used, so try to make your ad as economical as possible. Use the abbreviations that you learned when you were looking for cars to buy.

4. Paste your ad inside the front cover of your project folder.

> **EXTENSION:** Call a local newspaper and ask for the rates they charge for an ad of this type. Calculate how much it would cost you to run your ad for a week in your local newspaper. Write up a bill for running your ad. Include it in your project folder.

Resale Worksheet

Name _____

Fill in the blanks below.   *Show your work below.   Write dollar amounts on this side.*

Price You Paid for Your Car: _____

Deductions –

_____ _____
age of the car
(Deduct 4% per year owned.)

_____ _____
mileage
(Deduct 1% per 12,000 miles.)

_____ _____
accidents
(Deduct 5% per accident.)

Total Deductions: _____

Credits +

_____ _____
maintenance
(Good? Add 3% for careful maintenance.)

_____ _____
special features
(Add 2% for special features you have added.)

Total Credits: _____

Resale Price of Your Car: _____

(Subtract total deductions from price you paid. Add credits.)

Car Buyer's Project • Self-Evaluation

Name _____

1. What math did you learn for the first time, learn more about, or practice during this project?

2. What did you like best about this project?

3. What would you change about this project?

4. What math in this project do you think you know well?

5. What math in this project do you think you need to learn more about?

Car Buyer's Project •
Grading Your Own Work

Name _____

In grading this project, your teacher will be looking closely at the following:
1. Is the math accurate?
2. Is the budget reasonable and balanced?
3. Is the Lifestyle Essay thoughtful and creative?
4. Is every part of the project complete?

In the space below, please grade yourself on your project. Give yourself a grade in each category and briefly explain why that grade is appropriate.

My math calculations:

My budget:

My Lifestyle Essay:

How I dealt with the hard parts of this project:

Toothpaste Shareholder's Math–1   Name _____

You own 100 shares of Rufus Mayflower's Toothpaste Company stock.
You made a data chart to track the company.

	close	net change
Monday	$1\frac{2}{8}$	$+\frac{1}{8}$
Tuesday	$1\frac{3}{8}$	$+\frac{1}{8}$
Wednesday	$1\frac{4}{8}$	$+\frac{1}{8}$
Thursday	$1\frac{5}{8}$	$+\frac{1}{8}$
Friday	$1\frac{6}{8}$	$+\frac{1}{8}$

Week 1

1. At what price, in dollars, did the stock close on Monday?
   Describe two ways to figure out the worth of your stock on Monday.

2. Suppose that at the end of last week the stock was trading at 17/8.
   Has the value of your shares gone up or down?
   How much more or less is your stock worth at the end of this week?
   Explain how you figured out your answer. <u>Show all equations</u>.

Toothpaste Shareholder's Math-2

Name _____

Mrs. Losq has $1,000 to invest. Her broker told her about this dynamite toothpaste company. Mrs. Losq decided that since everybody uses toothpaste she would invest. She decided to track the company for a week to find a good investment moment.

Week 2

	close	net change
Monday	$2\frac{4}{8}$	$+\frac{6}{8}$
Tuesday	$2\frac{1}{8}$	$-\frac{3}{8}$
Wednesday	$3\frac{3}{8}$	$+1\frac{2}{8}$
Thursday	$3\frac{4}{8}$	$+\frac{1}{8}$
Friday	$2\frac{5}{8}$	$-\frac{7}{8}$

1. How many shares could Mrs. Losq have bought for $1,000 on Monday?
   Explain how you figured out your answer. <u>Show all equations.</u>

2. On which day should she have bought into the company? Why? How many shares would her $1,000 have bought on that day?
   Explain how you figured out your answer. <u>Show all equations.</u>

3. Mrs. Losq decided to buy on Friday. How many shares can she buy?
   Explain how you figured out your answer. <u>Show all equations.</u>

4. Make a line graph showing the performance of the toothpaste stock over two weeks. Find the first week on **Toothpaste Shareholder's Math-1**, S-29. The second week is on this page.

Did Your Stock Grow in Value?

Name _____

COMPARE PRICES

On a separate sheet of paper, convert all fractions to dollars and cents.

1. The first day I tracked my stock, its price was _____.
2. The last day I tracked my stock, its price was _____.
3. My highest price over the last month was _____.
4. My lowest price over the last month was _____.

MAKE A LINE GRAPH

Make a line graph showing your stock's movement over the last month. Draw the X-axis and the Y-axis, and then plan your graph.

1. Compare your low price and your high price. This will tell you your range for the Y-axis (vertical axis) of your graph. Decide what numbers will fit on your paper. Label this axis **Price per Share of (Name of Company) Stock**. Example: Price fluctuates from $28.50 to $31. Start the graph at $28 and end it at $32. Fit this on your paper. Divide your graph into $0.25 increments.

2. For your X-axis (horizontal axis) decide how many entries to include. Label this axis **Dates**. Example: Did you track your stock for 20 days? Put 20 lines on the axis, one for each date you will write. Space them evenly on the page.

3. Write in each date on the X-axis. Then use numbers you have written on your **Stock Recording Sheet**. Make a mark at the correct place for each date. Then use a ruler to draw lines between the marks. Label your graph **Prices of (Name of Company) Stock from (first day) to (last day)**.

INVEST $1,000

On a separate piece of paper, answer these questions. Show all equations.

1. If you invested $1,000 in the stock the first day, how many shares would you own?

2. How much would your investment be worth the last day you tracked the stock? (If your stock's value remained the same, do the CHALLENGE.)

3. CHALLENGE: Look up your stock's dividend (under Div. in the newspaper).
The company will pay you this amount per year for each share of the stock you own. How much will you earn in dividends this year?

4. For everybody: How would you rate your stock as an investment? Would you recommend it to a friend?

Mini-Portfolio   Name _____   Date _____

WHAT YOU NEED:

- your completed Ants' Picnic worksheet
- activity sheets for "Picturing Decimals, Fractions, and Percent"
- game recording sheets
- budgets from the Car Buyer's Project
- graph from the Stock Market Project
- "What I Already Know About Decimals" essay

1. Review the teacher's comments on your Ants' Picnic worksheet. Respond to the questions or suggestions. Then write a short paragraph describing what you learned from this activity.

2. Make a list of all the games, worksheets and activities you completed in this unit. Rate the activities from your favorite to your least favorite.

    Then write a short paragraph (at least three sentences) to explain what you learned from one of these activities.

3. Reread your essay, "Write About Decimals" and then think about what you know now. Describe three new things that you learned.

4. Respond to one of the following:

    One really amazing thing about decimals is . . .

    or

    With decimals, I think I'll need to learn more about . . .

    (As you respond, think about some of these questions: Did you learn new things that surprised you? What connections do you see between decimals, fractions, and percent? Does anything about decimals still confuse you? What else do you think you'll need to understand about decimals to be really confident?)

EXTRA CHALLENGE:

Use a calculator to solve these multiplication problems. Then explain why each answer makes sense. (HINT: You may find it helpful to think about fractions that are equal to some of these decimals.)

　　a.　4.12 x .25　　　　b.　4.12 x 2.5

How would you solve these problems without a calculator?